THIS TOO
SHALL PASS

June Eaton

Marie D. Jones

Carol Stigger

Publications International, Ltd.

June Eaton is a teacher and freelance writer whose published work includes Sunday school curriculum as well as stories and articles in more than 50 Christian publications. She has also contributed to many books, including *The Bible: A to Z, Prayers for Life,* and *A Mother's Daily Prayer Book.*

Marie D. Jones is an ordained minister and a contributing author to numerous books, including *Echoes of Love: Sisters, Echoes of Love: Friends, A Mother's Daily Prayer Book,* and *Book & Journal: Blessings.*

Carol Stigger is an award-winning communications consultant, a writing teacher, and a freelance writer. Her inspirational work appears in several national magazines, including *Guideposts, Vital Christianity,* and *Providence Journal.* She is also the author of *Opportunity Knocks.*

Louis Weber, CEO
Publications International, Ltd.
7373 North Cicero Avenue
Lincolnwood, Illinois 60712

Permission is never granted for commercial purposes.

ISBN-13: 978-1-4508-6046-8
ISBN-10: 1-4508-6046-X

Manufactured in China.

8 7 6 5 4 3 2 1

Library of Congress Control Number: 2012942589

Contents

Follow the Light of Faith

"Into each life some rain must fall." These words by Henry Wadsworth Longfellow speak one of life's basic truths. Sometimes, though, it seems the rain becomes relentless, perhaps even destructive. We get mired in pain and despair that threaten to derail us from our intended track of good health, success, and happiness. Suddenly, we feel lost and afraid. Absorbed in our suffering, we are unable to see the light beyond the clouds and begin to lose faith, wondering if we will ever experience joy again.

When this happens, we must take heart. No suffering lasts forever, and no pain continues unabated, especially when we call upon the infinite care and grace of a merciful God to help us get through. God reminds us to always look upward and have faith, for just as the clouds eventually drift away, revealing clear skies, so too will our anguish and hopelessness: "I will both lie down and sleep in peace; for you alone, O Lord, make me lie down in safety" (Psalm 4:8).

Within the pages of *This Too Shall Pass*, you will find prayers, stories, quotations, and poems designed to give you the warm sun and blue skies of healing and happiness you seek. This special book touches on many facets of the human experience: overcoming great challenges to the physical body; turning personal tragedy into triumph; learning lessons of patience, gratitude, and courage; and being restored by newfound hope, joy, and inner peace.

Ten chapters provide you with the wisdom and experience of those who have suffered through life's trials and made it to the other side. In every story, a ray of hope shines for those now struggling with their own pain and loss. This hope promises that after every storm there is always a beautiful rainbow arcing across the sky.

From the courageous task of moving through physical and emotional pain to the bountiful promises of prayer to change lives, *This Too Shall Pass* offers inspiring lessons for the heart and spirit to embrace. Let this book be a gift of comfort for you or for someone you love who is going through a difficult time—a gift promising that, with faith, hope, and the grace of a loving God, this too shall pass.

CHAPTER 1

Moving Through Pain

*G*od of my heart, I call to you in my suffering, asking for your healing grace. Teach me to have faith and to remain strong in the knowledge that, with you, I have the courage to face my pain and to move through it, no matter how hard it may seem. Amen.

To You I Give

Father in Heaven, to you I give my body, that you may heal it and restore it to perfection. To you I give my soul, that you may empower it and enable it to withstand all suffering. To you I give my mind, that you may sharpen it and renew it to see the positive. To you I give my spirit, that you may refresh it and enlighten it to rise above my physical ailment. To you I give my life, that you may mold and shape it to your will for what is best for me. Thank you, Father, for giving me a body, a soul, a mind, a spirit, and most of all, a life. Amen.

Incline your ear, O Lord, and answer me, for I am poor and needy. Preserve my life, for I am devoted to you; save your servant who trusts in you. You are my God; be gracious to me, O Lord, for to you do I cry all day long. Gladden the soul of your servant, for to you, O Lord, I lift up my soul. For you, O Lord, are good and forgiving, abounding in steadfast love to all who call on you. Give ear, O Lord, to my prayer; listen to my cry of supplication. In the day of my trouble I call on you, for you will answer me.

Psalm 86:1–7

This Too Shall Pass?

God, people often say, "This too shall
pass," but it really doesn't help much
when I'm in the thick of it. My pain is
sometimes too much to bear, and I long
to give you my burden and lighten my
load. You once promised you would take
it, didn't you? You promised to take my
yoke upon your shoulders. So here, God,
I surrender my pain to you. I must admit
that just saying those words makes my
pain seem a little easier to bear.
In fact, I am becoming more and more
convinced that I feel better today than
I did yesterday—even if it's just a
little bit better. This, too? You're making
a believer out of me, God.

Therefore you too have grief now; but I will see you again, and your heart will rejoice, and no one will take your joy away from you.

John 16:22 NASB

When, God, When?

Each day seemed harder to deal with than the one before it. Janice wondered if her chronic facial pain would ever diminish and if she would ever be able to play outside with her two small children again. It had been only three weeks since she was diagnosed with a severe sinus infection that was the result of a smaller infection having gone untreated. Her doctor had prescribed two different drugs, but so far there was no relief, and it hurt Janice to even smile or stand by the window. The mere hint of sunlight was enough to make her eyes want to leap out of her skull. The intense pain behind them was building to a point where she wondered if she should wear sunglasses in the house.

Already, she had missed enough work to warrant losing several great new accounts her advertising agency had attracted. Janice's boss was being understanding, but if this went on any longer, he had made it known to her that he might have to replace her. She begged him to reconsider, assuring him that she was doing all she could to get better. On top of the agony that gripped her face and sinuses, she now had the fear and anxiety of being unemployed. With two small children to feed, that would be disastrous.

Fortunately, her mom was able to come and care for the boys while Janice went from doctor to specialist, from MRI to acupuncture, from yoga to massage therapy. She was willing to try anything and everything to relieve the pain, especially after learning from a specialist that she was going to require surgery to open up her severely blocked sinus ducts.

Janice did not want surgery. She could not afford to take the additional time off work and be away from her boys. There was no guarantee that it would even work to diminish the pain, because there was always the threat of the infection returning. Something inside her told her to keep looking for a solution, that there was something she could do to help herself.

Without anywhere to turn, Janice did something she had rarely had the time or the inclination to do before. She went into her bedroom, closed the door, and prayed to God for healing. Her prayer began with an apology, for she felt her own complaints were small compared with the trials of others who were dealing with tragic diseases such as cancer and AIDS. But still she felt compelled to share her suffering with God, and the feeling washed over her that she indeed was cared for, no matter how small her pain was compared with that of others.

After Janice prayed, she felt better, enough to give her hope. She began to pray more often, especially when the pain was unbearable and the medications failed to work quickly.

It happened slowly, but it did happen. Two weeks later, Janice woke up feeling absolutely no pressure in her head or around her eyes. She sat up, almost waiting for the pain to return, but it never did. That day she rediscovered the simple joys of being well: getting dressed and hugging her boys, going to work, and coming home and cooking dinner.

She went back to the doctor, who scheduled another MRI, and Janice discovered that the blockage and swelling had gone down a great deal. She already knew that, of course, because she had her life back.

Janice realized much of the pain had been amplified by her own anxiety and the tension she herself created with each episode, and she learned how to become quiet and pray whenever she felt the pressure returning. The pain did

return, but it was not nearly as bad as before.
Each time, she prayed it away, knowing that what
doctors could not do for her God could and
would. And for that she would always be grateful.

*B*lessed One, I know there are others in
the world in far more desperate situations
than I am, but still I need your help.
This challenge is testing my faith, my
patience, and my courage, and I cannot
do it without a higher power at my side.
Be there for me, when I am feeling at my
worst, to reveal to my tired eyes the joys
that await me when I am healed. Thank
you, God.

*N*o pain, no palm; no thorns, no throne; no gall, no glory; no cross, no crown.

WILLIAM PENN, "NO CROSS, NO CROWN"

*H*ear my prayer for healing, Lord, that
I may walk in the light of wholeness
once again.
Hear my prayer for freedom from pain,
that I may move with the grace and
ease of a dancer.
Hear my prayer for renewal of spirit, that
I may feel more empowered than ever
before.
Hear my prayer for physical strength, that
I may be able to work again.
In gratitude and love, hear my prayer.
Amen.

*W*hat is required to move through suffering? The will to do so and the inner strength to carry on when the body would rather give up entirely. We must also have hope and the deeply felt belief that all will turn out well. We must have faith—not in our own ability to rise above challenges, but in God—for our faith is what keeps us going. And we must have patience, for sometimes God's timing is not our own, and there are lessons we must first learn before we can truly be healed. Finally, we must have love—for ourselves and even for our pain—for in many ways, love is our teacher.

Lord, I Seek You

Lord, I seek you with all my heart,
with all the strength you have given me.
I long to understand that which I believe.
You are my only hope; please listen to
me. Do not let my weariness lessen my
desire to find you, to see your face. You
created me in order to find you; you gave
me strength to seek you. My strength and
my weakness are in your hands: preserve
my strength, and help my weakness.
Where you have already opened the door,
let me come in; where it is shut,
open at my knocking.
Let me always remember you,
love you, meditate upon you, and
pray to you, until you restore me
to your perfect pattern.

AUGUSTINE OF HIPPO

Back in the Game of Life

Lynne couldn't remember life without the agony caused by fibromyalgia. It seemed as though she had been suffering from the debilitating, chronic pain all her 45 years, although in reality the disease hadn't made itself known until five years ago. Still, the body aches and overwhelming fatigue had begun to take such a toll on her that Lynne felt certain she would never feel better again.

Having this disease meant not being able to enjoy normal things, such as grocery shopping or even walking with her neighbors. Lynne had recently discovered the Internet and online shopping, a welcome convenience for her. She could have needed items delivered to her door on days when the pain was incapacitating.

Sympathetic friends often gave Lynne suggestions and advice, everything from positive thinking to seeing a chiropractor. Lynne appreciated their concern, but they had no knowledge of the disease and its treatment. She often felt so alone in her suffering, despite the fact that more than 5 million Americans have the mysterious condition. She had tried many different treatments, from medications to warm-water therapy. Some had worked temporarily, but the meds left her with undesirable side effects and the pain returned in the end.

There were weeks at a time when Lynne felt so awful that she wondered whether life was really worth living. She had nothing tying her to this life—no husband or children—except for a job she loved as a graphic designer when she felt well enough to work. She never really thought seriously of suicide, but the idea of going to sleep one night and never waking up often tempted her when every cell in her body seemed to be on fire with agonizing pain.

Despite her misery and loneliness, Lynne never gave up. She couldn't. God had instilled in her a stubbornness that she used to dislike but now was grateful for. Something inside her was determined to overcome this challenge and find a life free from pain.

It was by divine intervention that Lynne

> **The Lamb at the center of the throne will be their shepherd, and he will guide them to springs of the water of life, and God will wipe away every tear from their eyes.**
>
> **Revelation 7:17**

discovered a new treatment for fibromyalgia. She had been feeling forlorn and forced herself to get out of the house and sit in a local bookstore coffee shop. At one point, she felt so fatigued she thought she would faint. She rose to leave, but something made her sit down again, so abruptly she almost spilled the iced tea she was holding. As she sat there, two women sat down at the table next to her. Lynne could not help but overhear them talking. One of the women had fibromyalgia and was raving about her success with CBT. On and on she gushed about how this CBT had helped her pain diminish to the point where she could now do all the things she did before.

Lynne listened, and as the women got up to leave, she rose and asked the woman what CBT was, explaining that she, too, has fibromyalgia. The woman explained that CBT was cognitive behavioral therapy and gave Lynne the name of a woman in town specializing in this treatment.

Without hesitation, Lynne made an appointment with the psychologist and began a long recovery of behavioral therapy that taught her to live with the pain and gave her tools to minimize it. And it worked, combined with a new exercise program Lynne felt good enough to undertake.

One year later, Lynne found herself somewhere she never thought she would be again—on a tennis court playing tennis. The pain was there, but it was a blur off in the distance as her body moved with an ease she hadn't known for several years. She stopped midgame and smiled, realizing for the first time that she had actually made it through the suffering she'd thought would never end. She had regained her life.

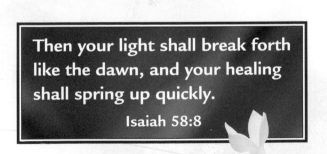

Then your light shall break forth like the dawn, and your healing shall spring up quickly.

Isaiah 58:8

*T*he experience of pain is always a catalyst for spiritual growth and expansion. What we endure becomes the opportunity to increase the power of our inner and outer strength.

Blessed are you who are hungry now, for you will be filled. Blessed are you who weep now, for you will laugh.

Luke 6:21

*G*od will never leave thee,
    All thy wants He knows,
    Feels the pains that grieve thee,
    Sees thy cares and woes.

Raise thine eyes to heaven
When thy spirits quail,
When, by tempests driven,
Heart and courage fail.

When in grief we languish,
He will dry the tear,
Who His children's anguish
Soothes with succour near.

All thy woe and sadness,
In this world below,
Balance not the gladness,
Thou in heaven shalt know.

General Hymn #286, Book of Common Prayer

Bending the Lord's Ear

Lord, it's me again, calling out to you,
for I am in pain and need someone to
talk to. I know that I should have courage
and fortitude and grit my teeth and bear
this pain, but it really helps me to have
someone to complain to, and if I can't
complain to you, dear Lord, well then
who *can* I complain to? For I know that
you will listen to my rantings and that
you will treat me with love, compassion,
and kindness, even as I am bending your
ear. Thank you, Lord, for the time,
for the attention, and for the care.
It really does help. Amen.

*G*od, in your presence I find the strength I need to carry on through these days and nights of pain and suffering. In your light I find the guidance and direction I seek to keep me on the path, looking forward with my face forever upward toward the sun. I know that my pain is transient, and I know that my suffering will end. Yet while I am immersed deep within it, your mercy serves as a soothing balm to lessen the aches, and your grace is the food for which my tired and weary soul hungers.

Hang On Tight

After the birth of her third child, Gina thought she had been through more pain than any woman could ever handle. The other two births had been tremendously difficult, but now she was facing a challenge she had not predicted.

Her third child had been breech and was born cesarean. The surgery had gone fine, and baby Andy was perfect from head to toe. But one day after the surgery, as Gina lay in the stuffy hospital room recovering, she began to hemorrhage. She was rushed into the operating room and told that her uterus had ruptured and surgery would be required immediately.

What could she do but agree to more pain, more recovery, and a longer stay in her stuffy hospital room? But what really broke her heart was the fact that she would not be able to nurse her son because the contractions caused by nursing would complicate her delicate condition.

After the surgery, Gina was in the most intense pain she had ever felt. Because she was given powerful medications, she was not nursing the baby, who would have been affected by any drugs in her milk. They deadened the pain but also made her feel like a zombie. Gina was unable to respond to her baby, and she began to suffer from postpartum depression and feelings of guilt and inadequacy as a mother. Between agonizing over her physical inability to even move off the bed and her inability to cuddle and nurse her new child, she slipped deeper and deeper into a dark place of sadness and anger.

With help from her husband, Rick, Gina found the strength to get through each day, but barely. It was not until a good friend came to visit that Gina found an outlet for her dark feelings and her pain.

Linda had been through a similar ordeal five years earlier, and she sat by Gina for two days straight, talking and commiserating with her. She encouraged Gina to do something that she herself had done in the depths of her most troublesome pain: surrender the situation to God and pray for relief.

Gina felt too tired and drugged to do much praying, but she was so down she felt she had nothing to lose. So she prayed in those silent moments when Rick was asleep and the baby lay nestled in the bassinet by her hospital bed. She gazed at Andy, longing for the time when she could be a real mom, a hands-on mom, and she prayed and prayed.

Praying did wonders to help Gina, and before long she was up and moving around the room, even venturing out into the hallway for brief strolls past the nurses' station. Her greatest joy came from being able to hold Andy and give him his bottle. The lactation nurse told her she could possibly still nurse Andy and gave her information on pumping until she was off the antibiotics and pain medicines. It might be hard, the nurse told her, now that Andy was used to the bottle, but the possibility alone kept Gina hanging on tight until one day she got word that she could go home.

> **Daughter, your faith has made you well; go in peace, and be healed.**
>
> **Mark 5:34**

Her praying didn't end then. She continued to ask for the divine guidance she needed for her recovery. She even began nursing Andy. Although it was tough going at first, the hard work was worth the result.

Gina could now be the hands-on mom she wanted to be, thanks to the help of loved ones, especially Rick and her friend, Linda, who had never given up on her and who gave her the faith to keep hanging on. With their help and the help of a little divine intervention, Gina blossomed into a mom with a mission. She was determined to help other mothers suffering in postpartum hell. She would use her experience, strength, and hope to help these women find the courage to make it through the pain.

*L*ord, my friends and family have been a wonderful support, but even they cannot take this pain from me. Only you, dear Father, can remove my burden and my suffering. Only you, dear God, can take away my deepest despair and replace it with a newfound strength and a renewed appreciation for my life. I surrender my will and my life to you, dear Spirit, that you may do your wondrous works in me. Amen.

*I*f someone you love is in pain, the best gift you can give them is your time and your caring attention. Listen as they talk, for great relief often comes from the simple act of getting our feelings out in the open. Help them with simple chores, make their lives a little bit easier, and do nice things to help keep them smiling through their suffering. Most of all, keep them from giving up, no matter how bad the pain gets. Remind them that this too shall pass and that one day they will awaken to the wonderful feeling of wholeness again.

One Step at a Time

Lord, I can do this. I can get through this day, one step at a time, one moment at a time. With you as my strength, I can do this. I can make it through another long, hard day, one ache at a time, one hurt at a time. For I am more than this body, and I am greater than this pain. With you as my strength, I can overcome any obstacle and surmount any challenge. For this I am grateful, Lord. For this I am able to carry on.

The Lord sustains them on their sickbed; in their illness you heal all their infirmities.

Psalm 41:3

*F*ather, I know that pain is an opportunity, but could you please find an easier way to teach me my life lessons? This suffering is taking a toll on me, and I have no choice but to reach out to you for help, for I cannot do it alone. I am willing to see where my suffering takes me, God, and I am willing to be patient and await my day of healing. I only ask that you be there with me each step of the way. Amen.

Keep On

*I*n the midst of suffering
I know I'm bound to find
the seeds of opportunity
to strengthen body, soul, and mind.

Within the darkest hours
There's a ray of hope ahead,
and if I follow faithfully,
to God I will be led.

When my body aches with pain,
and there is no end in sight,
I keep my eyes upon the prize
and keep on moving toward
    God's light.

Let Me, Lord

Fill me with the power of your presence, Lord, that I might be an angel to someone who is suffering today. Teach me compassion for those who may be in pain, that I might understand how best to fill their needs. Let me be a caretaker to some sad and despairing soul, for my light is strong and my faith is solid. Let me be a guide to someone who is lost and alone, for I know with sureness the path my feet tread upon. Amen.

Signposts

The sadness felt like a tidal wave that threatened to drown Vera. Her medication was simply not working, and she was reluctant to continue popping pills when already three other antidepressants had failed to help her. She had been through three psychiatrists, two ministers, and several alternative healers, yet no one could seem to make Vera's dark depression lift.

Perhaps it was the shame of having the disease in the first place that weighed Vera down so heavily. Despite the fact that depression was a widespread epidemic in America, claiming more victims each year, she still regarded it as the "black sheep" disease, the one nobody likes to talk about.

Her inability to enjoy her life had already cost her a marriage, and yet she still could not seem to will herself to be happy. Deep down inside, she knew it had nothing to do with will, but she continued to try, waking up each morning determined to think positive and be cheerful. It never worked. Come midday, the black cloud of despair would settle over her and smother any positive thoughts that might have been budding in her mind.

Vera's family suspected she was having problems, but none of them had any idea of the extent of her mental illness. They did not know of her suffering, her anxiety, her shame, and her hopelessness. They did not understand that because of her depression she had gained a lot of weight, lost a lot of friends, and stopped going out of the house unless absolutely necessary.

Vera lived alone, so no one was around to notice her growing lack of interest and apathy toward life. But *she* knew, and she was silently crying out for help if only someone would listen.

It began to feel as though the heavy clouds would never lift. That's when Vera began to think about her options in stark reality. She could either give in to the depression and die as a result, or she could continue to fight. She wanted to continue to fight, but she didn't have any strength left in her. That realization made her sadder than anything, and it made her terribly afraid.

Backed into a corner, Vera did what most human beings do when there are no options left. She got down on her hands and knees, literally, and prayed to God. She prayed for a sign that would point her toward healing. She prayed for laughter. She prayed for a morning when she would awake without despair creeping up on her like a poisonous snake. She prayed for help and understanding, in whatever form God chose to deliver it.

The next morning, Vera felt depressed, but something was different. She had a sense of resolve, to get through this trial and come out whole and healed. It was a small sense of resolve, but as she went about her day, it grew more and more pronounced.

Three days later, Vera was at her doctor's office, discussing a new drug on the market. She was willing to try it, along with a more intensive therapy the doctor recommended. She was willing to try anything, not because she was desperate but because she believed that God helps those who seek his help and that healing angels often come to us in the form of doctors and therapists.

The path now laid before Vera was not an easy one. It was rife with days that were as dark as any she had ever experienced and nights that threatened to swallow her whole. But her spirit had been made stronger through prayer, and she continued to talk to God each night, asking for guidance. More important still, she followed that guidance each day and took the necessary steps toward her recovery.

Vera began the new medication and the new therapy. Almost immediately she felt an improvement in her mental and physical well-being. Not a big leap, but a small step, enough to keep her going forward, seeking each signpost left along the way for her by God.

So we do not lose heart. Even though our outer nature is wasting away, our inner nature is being renewed day by day. For this slight momentary affliction is preparing us for an eternal weight of glory beyond all measure.

2 Corinthians 4:16–17

*W*hen the body is imprisoned by pain, it is hard to think of the joys of life without bitterness and resentment.

> The Lord will guide you continually, and satisfy your needs in parched places, and make your bones strong; and you shall be like a watered garden, like a spring of water, whose waters never fail.
>
> **Isaiah 58:11**

Trapped by the limitations of our physical suffering, we begin to wonder if we will ever be able to do something as simple as climb a staircase again. But we do not have to suffer alone. We can turn to the medical community for assistance. We can turn to friends, family, and support groups for concern and sympathy. We can turn to others in pain for empathy and advice. And we can turn to God and pray for healing.

Then we await that healing with a joyful
expectancy, for God never turns away
from a heartfelt prayer for help.

The Life that Gives Life

*H*oly Spirit, the life that gives life.
You are the cause of all movement;
You are the breath of all creatures;
You are the salve that purifies our souls;
You are the ointment that heals our
     wounds;
You are the fire that warms our hearts;
You are the light that guides our feet.
Let all the world praise you.

HILDEGARD OF BINGEN

CHAPTER 2

The Power of Surrender

*H*ave no fear for what tomorrow may bring. The same loving God who cares for you today will take care of you tomorrow and every day. God will either shield you from suffering or give you unfailing strength to bear it. Be at peace then, and put aside all anxious thoughts and imaginations.

ST. FRANCIS DE SALES

*D*ear God, help me surrender my busy schedule and endless lists to your wiser plan. Show me what I can give up so I will have time for the things that count. Time to worship, time to pray, time to watch a leaf drift lazily to the grass. Time to prepare a meal from scratch with unhurried hands. Time to read a book to a child. Time to comfort a friend. Remind me, Lord, that ticking clocks and calendars were not created by your holy hands. Amen.

An Extra Measure

Lead me gently today, Lord, through the
moments when I may fail to trust that
you are beside me. Remind me that no
path is too twisted for you to straighten,
no heart is too sore for you to heal, and
no problem is too big for you to solve.
Give me an extra measure of faith today
so I can glimpse the bright beauty at
the end of this road, and give me an
extra measure of courage for the journey.
Thank you for walking with me
every step of the way.

*F*ather, you have an answer for every question, a solution for every problem, forgiveness for every sin, and love through all eternity. The magnitude of your gifts overwhelms me, yet at times I feel forgotten and alone. Please enlarge my limited understanding so I may know your grace in every moment and never feel I am in this by myself. Forgive my lapses in faith, and help me learn the difference between *knowing* you are here and *feeling* you are here. With your help, my feelings will not become more important than what I know to be true. Amen.

Growing Older with a Grimace and a Grin

Helen's daughter Cindy and one-year-old grandson Cameron were visiting. To give them more space, Helen had put them in her bedroom and slept on the sofa bed. Maybe that's why all her joints ached. Or was it because she could not resist sweeping her grandson into her arms every time she turned around? She was getting better at walking around his toys instead of stumbling over them and had stopped being startled every time a toy chattered, oinked, or burst into song. Things had changed since her children were young. Toys, even books, talked, squawked, or barked back.

Cindy kept the TV volume so low that Helen told her to turn on the closed-captioned feature. Her daughter frowned and told her she could hear every word. When Helen couldn't find her eyeglasses, Cindy found them for her. They didn't talk about the plastic denture container in the bathroom or Helen's expanding collection of prescription drugs.

However, she heard Cindy talking to her brother Ted on the phone. "Mom's got old lady syndrome," she said. She was striving for humor but sounded concerned.

When Helen's son arrived for dinner that night, he repaired the porch light, fixed a mini blind, and replaced a ceiling lightbulb—things Helen had asked him to do a month ago. Then, Ted swept the light dusting of snow from the sidewalk, explaining he was concerned, "You could slip and break a hip." Meanwhile, Helen's daughter told her to sit down and cut up the salad ingredients while she prepared the stroganoff, Helen's signature dish.

"Aren't you afraid I'll cut myself with this big sharp knife?" Helen was trying to joke, but a slight snarl curdled the humor. Still, it was nice to sit down at the table with Cameron, who was in his high chair rubbing a banana in his hair. He dropped his cup. "Uh-oh," Helen said. "Uh-oh," he echoed with his five-tooth grin. Helen picked up his cup. "Uh-oh," he said and dropped his spoon. They played the "uh-oh" game so long that Cindy graciously finished making the salad while Ted set the table.

Their conversation was less interesting than Cameron's journey into the land of self-feeding. "I have to have a root canal," Helen's son said. *My dentures will never decay*, Helen thought, watching Cameron squash a pea with his thumb.

"I'm trying to figure out how to set up Cameron's college fund," Helen's daughter said. *Been there; done that,* Helen thought. Cameron held a pea over the side of his chair. "Uh-oh," Helen said. The pea rolled across the floor. Her children, deep in conversation about finances and insurance, ignored them. She noticed that they both had lovely table manners.

Cameron would, too, eventually. "Uh-oh." His spoon hit the floor. Helen bent to pick it up. "Uh-oh!" he cried. She sat up with an apple slice dangling from her hair. He executed a smooth maneuver: a spoonful of peas into his mouth. Helen clapped her hands. Cameron clapped his sticky hands. His mother and uncle moved on to a discussion of mortgage rates. *My house is paid off, hooray!* thought Helen. Cameron played peekaboo with his plate. She caught the plate before it hit the floor. He swirled the food on his tray with a finger and laughed. "Gmmmopf," he said, holding out his little arms.

"Mom, do you think I should refinance my condo?" Cindy asked offhandedly.

"Did you hear that?" asked Helen, smiling. "He said 'Grandma!'"

"Huh? He's a mess! Do you think I could get a better interest rate?"

"All I know is this boy needs a bath." Helen extracted Cameron from the high chair and carried him into the bathroom. Soon he was splashing water out of the tub with glee. A tugboat sang a sailing song. Her glasses steamed up. Her shirt dripped. Her knees hurt, and her back ached. She sang along with the tugboat. In the kitchen, her children discussed grown-up things. In the bathtub, a precious child reached out his arms. He was most definitely saying "Grandma" . . . minus a few key vowels and consonants. A smile sat gently on Helen's heart.

*G*row old along with me!
   The best is yet to be,
   The last of life, for which the first
      was made;
   Our times are in His hand
   Who saith, "A whole I planned,
   Youth shows but half; trust God:
   See all, nor be afraid."

ROBERT BROWNING

We do not live to ourselves, and we do not die to ourselves. If we live, we live to the Lord, and if we die, we die to the Lord; so then, whether we live or whether we die, we are the Lord's.

Romans 14:7–8

Our God of Surprises plants new things in our autumn gardens. Our complaints are the price of living to a ripe old age. Voicing regret over the natural decline in energy and the suppleness of our bodies is not ingratitude to God. He places a high value on truth. But it is ungracious not to look for the new joys he has prepared for us. Imagine being a teenager again: energy and enthusiasm but little wisdom. When the grandchildren begin arriving, one has the wisdom of decades of living *and* all the joy babies bring to our lives. Thanks be to God for all the lovely things we find "over the hill."

*A*ge is mandatory; wisdom is optional.

*B*egin to weave and God will provide
the thread.

GERMAN PROVERB

*D*ear God, please count me in when I say "count me out." Count me worthy when I feel worthless and count me blessed when I feel cursed. I know these bitter feelings pass with time, but time is going slowly. My sense of purpose is drifting away on a river of tears. Let me feel your gentle touch today, reminding me that I can count on you even when I can't count on myself.

New Day

As I unwrap your gift of this new day,
heavenly Father, I ask you to open my
eyes to beauty, open my ears to joy, open
my mouth to praise, and open my heart
to love. Forgive me for the days when I
left your gifts upon a shelf, reluctant to
receive them. This is a *new* day, Lord, and
with your help I will live it fully. Amen.

Beside the Pond

Alzheimer's disease draped cobwebs over Uncle
Bill's mind, and the day came when he no longer
recognized his nephew, Jim. Soon he forgot his
children, and then his wife, who cared for him so
patiently and tenderly. "Who are these people?"
he asked at a family dinner, nervously directing
his question to a bare corner of the room. In the
silence that followed, it was clear that those who
loved him most could not part the cobwebs with

words or actions. In the bosom of his family, Bill was lost and alone.

He was a soldier decorated for bravery, a poet whose slim little books sat on Jim's bookshelf, a father who had raised his children with wisdom and tenderness. He was the holder of memories of Jim's mother and grandparents who had died years ago. Now Bill's gifts of wisdom, courage, poetry, and memory were beyond his relatives' reach, like fragile treasures tucked away in a lost trunk. He had written his last poem, shared his last family story. He would never tell another child: "Don't run from fear; turn around and face it."

And Jim could never tell Uncle Bill that his poems had given him the courage to write poetry, that his family stories helped heal Jim's grief over his mother's death. Jim could never explain that, thanks to his teaching that was never preaching, he no longer ran from fear, but vanquished it by facing it. Now there was nothing Jim could give this man who had given so much to him. Bill did not know Jim's name or recognize his face.

After dinner, Jim put on his coat to take a walk. Uncle Bill said, "Hello," not "good-bye." Jim walked around the condominium complex. The day was brisk and cool but sunny. He walked through a small grove of trees thinking of the uncle he had known all his life, the uncle he did not know how to reach today. Jim came to a small pond. The antics of lively ducks smoothed the sharp edges of his sorrow. When his children were young, he had often taken them to feed the ducks. It was an activity they had enjoyed immensely.

Jim returned to the dinner table in time for dessert. His uncle ate hot apple pie with ice cream melting in puddles around it. Bill's napkin was neatly folded in his lap. He used the correct fork and poured the usual amount of cream in his coffee. But when he stood up, he did not say "excuse me." He bowed his head and said the family's table grace. "He still enjoys his food," said Jim's aunt. "But he won't remember what he ate."

Jim put on his coat. "He won't remember this, either," he said as he helped Bill put on his coat. Jim wrapped the leftover bread in a napkin and put it in his pocket. He held his uncle's hand like they were two little children. As they walked through the woods, Jim recited one of

Bill's poems. He stopped to stroke the bark of a tree. They watched a squirrel scurry into a hole. "What's that furry little thing?" Bill asked. Before Jim could answer, Bill plucked a golden leaf and handed it to him. "Who are you?" Bill asked, but he did not seem concerned. Jim answered by reciting another one of Bill's poems as they walked on.

They sat on a bench beside the pond. The ducks were still swimming and diving. Jim threw a small piece of bread in the pond, and the ducks descended on it in a flurry of feathers and quacks. He handed Bill a piece of bread. His uncle threw it in the pond and laughed when the ducks rushed to it. When the bread was gone, Jim took Bill's hand and said, "I am your friend and the keeper of your poems."

"Oh, why can't it be like it was!" is the cry of a soul in pain, a plea to God to make it better, and a deep longing to reclaim what we have lost. We cannot avoid the pain of grieving, for that is love's steep price. But with God's help, we can look reality in the face without falling apart. With God's love, we can find the grace in this painful reality and embrace it as part of our life. With God's guidance, we can walk this new path with confidence and strength.

There You Are

Lord, I trust in you to lead me down dark
paths with your never-wavering light.
I trust in you to love me through the
bleakest days and longest nights.
I trust in you to keep my pain from
turning into black despair. I trust in you to
keep alive the flame of hope.
I trust in you to teach me why things must
be as they are today.
I trust in you to keep me on course as you
do the planets and the stars.
When I feel there is nothing left to trust,
I turn around, and there you are.
Thank you for your constant love.
Amen.

I pray for patience, the gift of waiting expectantly for my prayers to be answered. I know the answer may not be what I want but what is best for me. Your "yes," God, will fill me with joy. Your "no" or "not now" may be difficult to bear, but I will learn an important lesson from it. Patience, they say, is a virtue, but it is one I am not learning well on my own. Please teach me patience with myself, with you, and with all I encounter. My journey through life will be smoother this way.

*A*ll I have seen teaches me to trust the Creator for all I have not seen.

RALPH WALDO EMERSON

*T*he gap between your problem and a solution is only the distance from your knees to the floor.

Do not worry about your life, what you will eat or drink...Is not life more than food...? Look at the birds of the air, they do not sow or reap or store away in barns, and yet your heavenly Father feeds them. Are you not much more valuable than they?

Matthew 6:25–26 NIV

Prayer to the Holy Spirit

Breathe in me, O Holy Spirit, that my thoughts may all be holy. Act in me, O Holy Spirit, that my work, too, may be holy. Draw my heart, O Holy Spirit, that I love but what is holy. Strengthen me, O Holy Spirit, to defend all that is holy. Guard me, then, O Holy Spirit, that I always may be holy. Amen.

ST. AUGUSTINE

The Little Tree

Darlene's husband died in October. By Christmas she was still too grief-stricken to decorate the house. The ornaments they had collected over their 30 years of marriage were stored in the attic. She knew that handling them would unleash new rivers of tears. Her son offered to get a tree and help her string the lights, but she could not bear seeing those symbols of celebration yet. Darlene knew the grandchildren would be disappointed, but she was just now becoming accustomed to the echoing emptiness of a once lively home.

She would observe just one tradition, passed down through the generations of her father's family. At midnight on Christmas Eve, she would light a bayberry candle to welcome the Christ Child. The candle would burn through the night, being placed in the sink for safety when they went to bed.

Darlene's Christmas shopping item was a bayberry candle, harder to find as each year passed. The mall was exploding with holiday sights and sounds, but to her every manger scene and Santa was like a match that would not light. The music reminded her that this season was not joyous but mournful for her. She would give her loved ones checks, because she could not bear extra trips through the throng of Christmas shoppers and jolly clerks.

Darlene visited her son a week before Christmas for their tree-trimming party, but her grandchildren's Christmas joy was poignant, not contagious. Their warm hugs were comforting but did not ease the ache inside her. The carols they sang fell flat on her ears, and the freshly baked cookies tasted like straw.

As her son walked Darlene to her car, she saw a small artificial tree on the garbage can. "Remember that?" he said. "It's from our little apartment before the kids were born." The limbs were twisted, and the tree lay flat. *Like me*, Darlene thought. She asked him to put the discarded tree in her car. As sad as the tree looked, she felt like she was letting go of a tiny bit of grief.

The next morning, Darlene straightened the little tree's limbs and tied it to a dead evergreen bush in her front yard. It looked fake and forlorn. To fill an empty hour, she popped corn and strung it on thread. Then she draped the popcorn strand around the tree. Later, when she looked out the window, she saw the tree had many feathered guests. Her little salute to the season was a hit with the birds. Perhaps she could let go of another sliver of grief.

At the grocery store the next day, she put a large box of candy canes in the cart. Each was tightly wrapped in cellophane. She knew they would last through sleet and look festive on the little tree.

Darlene called her grandchildren and told them to walk a block out of their way so they would pass her house on their way to school. "There's a surprise on a little tree for you," she said. It was something for her to look forward to. Their pleasure over the invitation brought a smile to her lips for the first time in months. When school was out, she laughed out loud to see how many friends had joined them to help themselves to candy canes. She invited the children inside for hot chocolate. The sticky cups they left behind were signs of hospitality and celebration. "My moment of Christmas was good," Darlene said to herself, "but now it is over."

> I can do all things through him who strengthens me.
>
> Philippians 4:13

On Christmas Eve, grief hit her as sharply
as it had in those first days of her bereavement.
Darlene wanted to take a pill and go to sleep,
but she would not be the first person in six
generations to leave the bayberry candle unlit.
After a tissue box of tears, midnight finally came.
She struck a match. The candle shone bright
in her dark living room. For the first time in
Darlene's life, it burned only for her.

Christmas comes in many ways, and that night
it came to Darlene, but not in the living room:
Christmas came by way of her little tree. The
bayberry candle, in a glass lantern, cast its golden
light on the shabby fake evergreen
and a few remaining candy canes.
Standing beside it outside, wearing
her husband's old coat, she said,
"Welcome, baby Jesus. The birds and
children have feasted here and left
you their sounds of joy. I bring you
all I have tonight, one small flame. It
is not much, but it is so much more
than I had just a moment ago."

Grief can be especially acute at Christmas when the decorations, parties, family traditions, and music further wound a broken heart. Christmas becomes a season to survive, not celebrate. "If I can just get through the holidays," people in mourning often say. But Christ, who came to us in a humble stable, will come to us no matter how barren our spirits or how deep our grief if we just give him a chance—if we trust him enough and take a little step toward Bethlehem.

I Give Up

Dear God, I give up. Take my burden.
It's stuffed with worry, dripping with
tears, torn with anger, and picked apart
by frustration. I have done everything I
can with it. I feel further away from the
answer than when I began, and I am so
incredibly weary of trying to deal with it.
I wanted to give you more, God, more
than this sorry lump of human care.
Maybe my pride got in the way. Or maybe
I did not want to bother you with it. But
you say, "Come to me all you who are
burdened and heavy laden, and I will give
you rest." Here I am, Lord, not just giving
up and quitting, but giving it up to you.
Amen.

*G*ive me a task to do today, Father. But do not tell me what it is. This way I may find the strength to meet each person and to unravel each problem like you handed it to me personally. I can run every errand and accomplish every chore as if I am doing it especially for you. Help me to learn that everything matters, everything counts, and to learn that each day lived is lived for your glory. Amen.

I will both lie down and sleep in peace; for you alone, O Lord, make me lie down in safety.

Psalm 4:8

*H*ave courage for the great sorrows of life and patience for the small ones; and when you have laboriously accomplished your daily task, go to sleep in peace. God is awake.

Victor Hugo

Behind the Clouds

As above the darkest storm cloud
Shines the sun, serenely bright
Waiting to restore to nature
All the glory of his light,
So, behind each cloud of sorrow,
So, in each affliction, stands,
Hid, an angel, with a blessing
From the Father in his hand.

DANIEL H. HOWARD

A Trip to the Holy Land

Charlotte loved to travel and liked to write, so
her dream was to be a travel writer. The perks
of traveling the globe on an expense account
were motivating: the white sand beaches of San
Tropez, Rio, Ambergris Caye…designer goggles
for Alpine slopes and Birkenstocks for Dolomite
hikes…Greece for culture, Provence for truffles,

and Italy for sculpture. She listed destinations and taped posters to her walls. In her years of writing corporate brochures in a cold building in a boring town, she had stared at her posters of moonlit lagoons and wept over scores of rejection letters from travel magazines. She tried hard and had talent but felt God was not giving her a single break.

Finally, she got an overseas writing assignment. It was not to cover a five-star resort for a magazine but to write about a mission for a charity. Charlotte did not tell the charity president that she had never known a poor person, was deaf to panhandlers, and was blind to shabby people holding handwritten cardboard signs. *This is my ticket,* she thought, *to glamorous assignments in more exciting places.*

She made a fool out of herself before she even packed her bags when she met the president of the charity.

He smiled and said, "You are going to the Holy Land."

Charlotte replied, "There's been a mistake. My tickets are for Haiti."

He just nodded and said, "You'll see."

What she saw when she reached Haiti was horrifying. Poor people slept in shifts for there was no room in their shanties for them all to lie down. Ditches of raw sewage with a hellish stench ran through an endless, sweltering slum. A retired dentist from Milwaukee ran the medical clinic. He weighed infants on a rusty produce scale and gave to the most critical cases formula and medicine from his sparse stores. A toddler vomited a worm on Charlotte's shoe. An infant died in her arms. She held its mother as the woman wept, and she dabbed the tears with her shirttail. She bought the child a soft little gown and a wooden coffin because the mother had no money and could not bury her child in dignity.

Charlotte was in the Holy Land, humbled by its poverty.

On her last day, the poor people she had befriended gathered to say good-bye. They had given her all they had—joy in their friendship and love. It was the greatest gift of her life, but they wanted to give Charlotte more. The bereaved mother handed her a basket she had woven. It held a ripe spotless mango, two fresh eggs, and a film canister filled with powdered milk.

Charlotte was in the Holy Land, humbled by its generosity.

Back home, she leafed through a travel magazine. The glitz and glamour of exotic resorts did not intrigue her. She wanted to go back to the Holy Land and write about the people nobody knows or cares about. God had finally answered her ten years of prayers to make her a travel writer, but he responded in a way she could not have imagined before she went to Haiti.

Now Charlotte has been to 30 countries. She has slept in bamboo huts and in crumbling little guesthouses with no addresses. She has worshiped in a church that had shower curtains for walls and the sky for a roof. She has broken bread with lepers and shared her granola bars with refugees. She has been welcomed by people speaking languages she'd never heard. In one African village, Charlotte shared a meal the women prepared in an old metal pot over an open fire. They ate with sticks. Something in that pot gave her dysentery, but the day they had spent together filled her spirit and still warms her heart. She has laughed and prayed and cried with some of the poorest

> **O how abundant is your goodness that you have laid up for those who ... take refuge in you, in the sight of everyone.**
>
> **Psalm 31:19**

people on earth. She has found that they are so rich in faith, love, and wisdom that she is honored and eager to write their stories.

And on every trip to the Holy Lands of God's poor, she is humbled by his plan for her.

*W*e all have a plan for our lives that is built on our dreams. We think we know ourselves well enough to make the best plan. This plan can turn into prayers. When they are not answered, we pray harder. Sometimes we lose hope. We may even wonder if anyone is listening. God's plan for our lives may not be our dream. His plan may be something we never imagined. Only when we let go of our dreams or ask God to reveal another plan can we live the life he is calling us to live.

Following You

Father, please help me stop trying to run my life and let you take charge. I know that your plans for me may be bigger and bolder than my plans, or they may seem smaller to me and less important. But I know that if I follow your will my life will be filled with the things that truly matter.

By following you, I will truly make a difference in our broken world, although I may never know the difference I have made. Thank you for calling me to your fields of labor and grace. I give you my longings and dreams. I give you my trust to reshape them according to your plan.

*H*elp me to understand, Lord, that simply by putting my hand in yours, I am blessed, protected, and led. I don't know where you will take me today, but I know I will need your guidance and protection. I think about how children reach up and take my hand with such trust. They know I won't let them stumble or wander into danger. Give me the trust of a child as we walk together today. Amen.

Prayer of Abandonment

*F*ather, I abandon myself into your
   hands; do with me what you will.
Whatever you may do, I thank you:
   I am ready for all, I accept all.
Let only your will be done in me,
   and in all your creatures—
I wish no more than this, O Lord.

CHARLES DE FOUCAULD

If I take the wings of the morning
and settle at the farthest limits of
the sea, even there your hand shall
lead me, and your right hand shall
hold me fast.

Psalm 139:9–10

CHAPTER 3

Beauty from Ashes

Lord, let me walk in the beauty of your creation, not in the ugliness of despair. Let me gaze upon the world with eyes that see everything as fresh and clean and new, not with eyes made cold and hard from negativity. Let me stand tall, face turned up toward heaven, not looking down at the ground in shame and weakness. Let me move with grace and ease and breathe freely, not imprisoned by pain and fear. Amen.

Let Me Rise

Lord, in the fire of my trials, let me rise
on wings of eagles to soar again. In the
depths of my depression, give me the
power to float upward toward the warm
sun where renewal and hope are found.
From the ashes of my suffering, let me
find the seed of new growth, of new life.
From the darkness of my despair,
let me be guided homeward by the light
of your love for me.

Beloved, do not be surprised at the fiery ordeal that is taking place among you to test you, as though something strange were happening to you. But rejoice insofar as you are sharing Christ's sufferings, so that you may also be glad and shout for joy when his glory is revealed.

1 Peter 4:12–13

The Rock

I rise like the phoenix from the ashes
    of my pain
And spread my wings to take flight
    once again.
With newfound wisdom, I rise into
    the sky,
And with clarity and focus, I shall fly
Higher than before, with greater
    ease,
For I have survived; I have achieved.
And when I come again to rest
    on land
Upon the rock of faith I will stand.

Picking Up the Pieces

"Bankruptcy." It was a word Linda had hoped she would never have to utter. But when she and her husband, John, talked to a lawyer about their financial situation, it seemed to be the only way out. They could either file for bankruptcy or risk losing everything, including their sanity, trying to figure out how to pay off the massive debt they had accrued.

Starting a home-based business had been the couple's dream for years. When they did put the pieces in place for their graphic arts company, they were sure they could make a success of it. Hard work and a long list of contacts gave them a boost at first. The jobs and money had poured in, but Linda and John had not been prepared for the feast-or-famine style of entrepreneurial life, and the months when they had income soon became outnumbered by the months when they had none.

As their debt mounted, Linda and John kept the faith and a positive attitude, taking out a second mortgage on their home to tap into their equity. They assumed they could find the clients to keep the business afloat and would be able to pay off any new debt in no time. They were wrong.

After the terrorist attacks of September 11, 2001, everything changed for the couple as people began to worry about the economy and their money. Disposable income shrank for many of their key clients, who had to make cuts wherever they could. Many chose to cut graphic design completely from their budgets.

As the months passed, Linda and John found themselves unable to keep up with the two mortgages, let alone other necessities such as health insurance, car expenses, and office supplies. Soon they received constant calls from creditors, and their once spotless credit report began to fill up with late notices and delinquent marks.

Filing for bankruptcy never crossed Linda's mind, but John had been discussing it with a lawyer friend. When he told Linda about it, she broke down and cried. To her, it would be an admission to the world that they had failed. John gently reminded her that, yes, their business had failed, but it was not the end of their lives.

Linda wanted more time to think about it. She considered asking her father for money, but that would have shamed her even more. Both her parents had warned her about the risks of self-employment. She did not want to hear them say "I told you so."

When the foreclosure notices from the banks started arriving, Linda and John realized it was time to face the reality of the situation. They filed for bankruptcy and went through the process with their lawyer. To their surprise, they learned there were many people just like them going through the same thing—people with broken dreams, people who had simply made mistakes. There was no shame in being human, the lawyer reminded them. The entire process lasted about six months and was not at all the horrifying experience Linda had imagined.

When their case was formally discharged, Linda and John felt a newfound sense of relief. They still had to find a way to pay their mortgages, but they had been able to discharge their credit card debt and lost only one of their two cars. Their credit was a disaster and would take years to repair. Still, they had come out of it alive and a little wiser for the wear and tear.

Both Linda and John decided to get full-time jobs, complete with benefits. Their dream of working for themselves was down for the count but only temporarily. They realized they had so much more to learn before they could venture out on their own. The bankruptcy had made them more responsible, more realistic, and more optimistic. It would be a long haul, picking up the pieces. They had lost a lot and learned a hard lesson or two about life, lessons they knew they would be grateful for further down the road.

*T*o endure is greater than to dare; to tire out hostile fortune; to be daunted by no difficulty; to keep heart when all have lost it; to go through intrigue spotless; to forego even ambition when the end is gained—who can say this is not greatness?

WILLIAM MAKEPEACE THACKERY

"*W*hatever does not kill us makes us stronger." Friedrich Nietzsche's statement is insightful, for is it not true that our trials serve to empower us in ways that our joys cannot? We meet with tribulation and suddenly find we have inner and outer resources we never imagined. Friends and loved ones come to our aid and care. They help us make a deeper connection to God, who carries us through the darkest nights of the soul when we cannot walk on our own. We survive intact, eager to live better lives than we had before. Whatever does not break us brings us closer to others, to ourselves, and to God.

Restore our fortunes, O Lord, like
the watercourses in the Negeb.
May those who sow in tears reap
with shouts of joy. Those who
go out weeping, bearing the seed
for sowing, shall come home
with shouts of joy, carrying their
sheaves.

Psalm 126:4–6

Insight

Father in heaven, I know that you work
in the most mysterious of ways and that
your greatest lessons are often shrouded
in the cloak of conflict and chaos.
Help me to discern your guidance in the
challenges I face and to recognize the
wisdom you offer in the obstacles placed
along my path. Give me an intuitive
heart and a perceptive soul that I may
see the buried treasures you have
intended for me to find.
Amen.

*D*ear God, fill me with the power of understanding and wisdom that I may learn from these situations what it is you desire to teach me. I know that from these times of despair and suffering great gifts can be discerned. Please give me this ability to discern, so your miracles and blessings are not lost upon my easily distracted mind. Open my heart to the possibilities my life can bring if I have faith. Empower and embolden me with the courage to get up when I am knocked down and to keep moving forward with the knowledge that you have a storehouse of joy awaiting me at the end of the bumpy road.

Finding Frieda

The car accident totaled Frieda's automobile, but what it did to her face totaled her spirit. She had been the beautiful one, the model with the perfect features and the $10,000-a-day look that advertisers sought. In fact, her career was about to gain another dimension with her first audition for a movie role, thanks to her ambitious agent. All this despite the fact that Frieda didn't really like modeling that much—it just paid too well to quit.

Lying in a hospital with half her face bandaged, Frieda wondered if she even had a life left to return to. She knew she did not have a career as a model anymore, and unless the movie role was for *The Bride of Frankenstein,* she figured she could kiss that opportunity good-bye.

What made the whole situation worse was knowing the accident was her fault. Frieda had not been paying attention to the road; she'd been busy talking to her agent on her cell phone. She never noticed the red traffic light until the SUV slammed into her car and sidelined her life.

It was easy for depression to take hold. Frieda's worth and identity had been centered around her looks. How could she possibly pick up the pieces and go on? The doctor told her plainly that the scars would be deep. Frieda was sure no amount of makeup could make them completely disappear.

Frieda's agent visited her and brushed off Frieda's concerns about her career, saying this was not the time to discuss it. She knew her agent was being polite, and she could clearly sense the older woman's resignation and disappointment. *No more chunky ten percent checks,* Frieda thought jadedly, *at least not from me.*

The days droned on, and Frieda spent her time in silence. Watching TV or reading magazines was too painful, what with the constant images of beautiful celebrities. She tried to read a novel, but the heroine was a "gorgeous lady" and that made Frieda feel sick inside. No one would ever call her "gorgeous" again.

On her final day in the hospital, a little girl came into Frieda's room by accident. Frieda sat up in bed and smiled. The child was in a wheelchair. She had no left arm, and her left leg was withered. Frieda felt such sympathy for the poor girl, until the girl opened her mouth.

Hallie was no victim. She was seven years old and definitely not shy. She wheeled right up to Frieda and said, "Hello," making it clear she was not going anywhere. Frieda was a little taken aback at the child's boldness but struck up a conversation with her. She learned that Hallie was going to have open-heart surgery in two days. Added to her disabilities and deformities, Hallie had a hole in her heart.

But again, Hallie was no victim. She was bright, funny, and bold, and she acted far wiser than her age. She spent the entire morning with Frieda, telling stories about her life and how she loved to spin her wheelchair in the hall and drive the nurses crazy. Not once did she complain about her situation. She was the happiest person Frieda had ever met.

> I will turn the darkness before them into light, the rough places into level ground. These are the things I will do, and I will not forsake them.
>
> **Isaiah 42:16**

When it was time for Frieda to be discharged, Frieda said good-bye to her new friend. As Hallie wheeled away down the hall, she turned back to Frieda and smiled, yelling, "Have a great life, friend!"

Three days later, Frieda called the hospital to ask if she could visit Hallie. The nurse sadly informed her that Hallie had not survived the surgery. Frieda hung up the phone and cried for hours. Then she gathered her wits about her and, with a resolve that surprised her, swore that she would "have a great life." Little Hallie's indomitable spirit would live on in Frieda's heart. She had no idea what that "great life" was going to be, but for the first time in a long time, she was inspired by the possibilities.

Comes the Light

From the dark night of the soul
   Comes the blessing of the dawn.
   From the deep wounds of the heart
   Comes the gift of love reborn.
   From the chaos of confusion
   Comes the calm of clarity.
   From the anguish of discord
   Comes the peace of harmony.
   From the grieving of great loss
   Comes the happiness of new life.
   From the coldness of despair
   Comes the warmth of our
      Father's light.

*W*hat makes a person beautiful? Is it just outside appearance or perfection of features and physical form? Perhaps there is a deeper beauty that comes from within, shining like a beacon that illuminates everyone and everything with which it comes in contact. This beauty is the glory of wisdom and courage, the power of inner strength and fortitude, the calmness of serenity and focus. This beauty comes from having faced life's biggest challenges and overcome them. This beauty comes from having known life's greatest sufferings and risen above them. This beauty is of one who has been born fresh from the ashes of hopelessness and the smoke of fear and now rises like a mighty angel poised to take flight.

Draw Me into Yourself

Draw me completely into yourself,

So that I might completely melt in
   your love.

Lay upon me, stamp upon me,

So that my stubborn pride might be
   destroyed.

Embrace me, kiss me,

So that my spiritual ugliness may turn
   to beauty.

Lock me into your chamber,

So that I might never stray from your
   presence.

JOHANN FREYLINGHAUSEN

Our Weakness, Your Strength

*T*here is much to drag us back, O Lord: empty pursuits, trivial pleasures, unworthy cares. There is much to frighten us away: pride that makes us reluctant to accept help; cowardice that recoils from sharing your suffering; anguish at the prospect of confessing our sins to you. But you are stronger than all these forces. We call you our redeemer and saviour because you redeem us from our empty, trivial existence, you save us from our foolish fears. This is your work, which you have completed and will continue to complete every moment.

SØREN KIERKEGAARD

Ashes to Angels

The fire raged across 500 acres, destroying everything in its path. The seasonal dry winds only served to fuel the beast, pushing waves of flames toward the small towns that bordered the forest.

Seventeen houses had been lost, and now Mary's house was in danger as the fire moved up the slope next to her backyard. The wind picked up sparks and ignited new fires every few yards. One spark landed on Mary's fence, and the fire quickly spread to the awning above her patio.

Within minutes, her home was engulfed in flames, despite the heroic efforts of firefighters and local civilians. From a hill across the valley, Mary watched as her life went up in smoke. She had been evacuated and taken what little she could with her to a friend's home. She'd brought her cat, family photos, and a few mementos of her late husband. That was all she could think of, her mind having been thrust into overdrive at the smell of the oncoming smoke. When she arrived at her friend Lucy's, she began to tremble, remembering things she should have taken with her and had left behind.

Now they were nothing but ash and rubble. The home she had made with the man she had loved since high school was gone. Stunned, and in a deep state of shock, Mary watched as her neighbors' homes went up in flames. A change in wind direction had turned the firewall, and the fire was heading into the deep valley that separated her lost home from the street where Lucy lived.

Mary helped Lucy and Lucy's husband, Phil, gather together what they could and get out before the fire cut off access to the one road leading to town. They drove quickly, in silence and in fear, as the wall of flames could be seen behind them making its way over the far slopes. Mary closed her eyes, too numb to feel anything. The drone of the car engine hypnotized her, and she fell asleep.

When Lucy awakened her, Mary found they were at the local shelter the Red Cross had set up at a school. Mary sat on a cot drinking coffee, watching the Red Cross volunteers help dozens of evacuees who filed into the room. She noticed several small children crying, clutching teddy bears and dolls, and wondered if they, too, had lost their homes. Watching this scene saddened her heart.

She had no idea what she would do next or where she would go. Lucy and Phil had offered their home for as long as she wanted, but at this point even they didn't know if they had a home. Mary thought about living with her daughter on the East Coast. She considered rebuilding, but mostly she just felt sick to her stomach at the thought of tomorrow, let alone today.

She shifted her focus to the Red Cross workers. They cared for everyone like angels, wrapping the children in blankets and providing hot drinks to those with hearts grown cold from the disaster. The more Mary watched, the more she began to realize she wanted to help. She wanted to get up, climb out of her depression, and offer herself to others in need. The desire surprised her, having never been a volunteer, but something inside her

> **For thus says the Lord: Just as I have brought all this great disaster upon this people, so I will bring upon them all the good fortune that I now promise them.**
>
> **Jeremiah 32:42**

seemed to come into sharp focus as she watched these volunteers.

I can do that, Mary thought over and over again. *I want to do that!* She set down her coffee and walked over to the welcome table. She offered her assistance, and the volunteers readily and happily accepted it. As Mary worked to get the newest evacuees settled in, her heart began to fill with hope and her spirit felt stronger. Her home was gone, but she had been blessed with many long and happy years there.

Now, she could either grovel in the ashes of her despair or become like the angels she saw moving about her. She chose to be an angel. Mary became a coordinator for the Red Cross in her county and went on to help hundreds of disaster victims find a reason to smile again.

*W*isdom is the ability to see beauty among the ashes of destruction and to know that from all endings new beginnings spring forth. We are always cared for, guided, and protected by God. Knowing this, we realize that when a door in our life slams shut, a window will open to give us new perspective and new opportunity. Our prayers never go unanswered, although the answers may not be what we expected. Yet, we are never abandoned, never alone. In our hearts, we know we can find good in the bad and positive in the negative. This is wisdom.

*I*nto thy hands, O Father and Lord, we commend this night, ourselves, our families and friends, all those we love and those who love us, all folk rightly believing, and all who need thy pity and protection: light us with thy holy grace, and suffer us never to be separated from thee, O Lord in Trinity, God everlasting.

ST. EDMUND RICH, ARCHBISHOP OF CANTERBURY

Help Them, God

God, help the weak and scared and make
them strong and courageous. I ask this
not for myself but for those in need,
for right now I have no complaints, no
problems. I ask this for those who cannot
see the light, those who are imprisoned
in the darkness of their ongoing despair.
Show them your glorious ways,
God, so they may come to know as I do
that there is good awaiting them around
the corner if only they believe.
Amen.

Living with Authenticity

For Robert, not being able to work meant not being able to be a man. As he was growing up, he had it hammered into him that being a real man meant working hard, even if it killed you. Robert's father had died fairly young of a heart attack, due to a stressful life filled with long, grueling hours on a job he never liked.

Robert never wanted to take a job just because it paid well. He wanted to acknowledge the gifts and talents he had been given. Yet here he was, in his late 30s, working as a supervisor at a power company, a job that drained him and left him too tired to enjoy his lovely wife, Sandy, and their four-year-old son, Mark.

Now, because of an accident on the job, Robert was on disability. His doctor told him he might never be able to go back to work. Sandy was sympathetic and said she would work to make up the lost income. He didn't want her to, knowing she preferred being at home with little Mark.

Sandy quickly found a job as a medical billing clerk at the doctor's office where she used to work. Robert spent his days at home with Mark, wondering what to do to turn his bleak future around. He could not walk without a cane. In fact, the only thing he was really good at, other than his job, was working with wood. He loved to design and build furniture, and their house was filled with chairs, tables, and knickknacks he had created in his spare time. His father had always scoffed at Robert's love of woodworking, reminding Robert that it was "just a hobby" and he should never think he could make a living at it. Like any obedient son, Robert had bought that edict hook, line, and sinker.

> **But for you who revere my name the sun of righteousness shall rise, with healing in its wings.**
> **Malachi 4:2**

But with money getting tighter and no options to speak of, Robert wondered if this injury may be a fantastic opportunity in disguise. Could he actually do something with his love of woodworking and even make a living at it?

He gathered the courage to ask his wife about it that night. Sandy thought it was a wonderful idea. She knew Robert was destined for something better than working until retirement at a job he hated. "What have we got to lose?" became their family motto, and Robert immediately set out designing small coffee tables and shelves. Sandy put some pieces up for auction on the Internet. She also registered for booth space at craft shows. Now it was do or die, and Robert worked day and night to get enough products ready to sell. He even let Mark help with the simple, safe tasks.

At the first craft show, they sold $5,000 worth of goods. Both Robert and Sandy were stunned. Thinking it may have been a fluke, they went to a swap meet and sold another $3,000 in one weekend. Then a few pieces were sold on the Internet, and they began to get orders from people who had seen the handcrafted wood pieces and wondered if Robert took custom orders.

Within one year, Robert was making almost as much money as he had on his old job. He worked hard, but he loved every minute of it, and that love showed in the quality time he set aside for his family. The house seemed brighter, filled with the joy that comes from living with authenticity.

The greatest gift of all for Robert was the lesson he was teaching his son, a lesson he wished his father had lived to learn: You can come back from a bad situation better and happier than before, and you can live your dream and earn a living by doing what you love.

*I*t is not in the still calm of life, or the repose of a pacific situation, that great characters are formed....Great necessities call out great virtues.

ABIGAIL ADAMS

*I*t is difficult in troubling times to imagine that any good can come from deep suffering. We are so caught up in our negative state that we cannot comprehend the idea of a silver lining. But some of life's greatest challenges lead to life's greatest lessons, lessons that bring about wisdom, maturity, and a newfound faith that did not exist before. Just as a lump of coal is transformed into a beautiful sparkling diamond only by submitting it to tremendous outer pressures, a life can be transformed into a joyful experience only by submitting it to opportunities for growth disguised as obstacles and challenges.

May you be made strong with all the strength that comes from his glorious power, and may you be prepared to endure everything with patience, while joyfully giving thanks to the Father, who has enabled you to share in the inheritance of the saints in the light.

Colossians 1:11–12

The Second Time Around

The pain of divorce permeated every part of Finola's life. She had signed the final papers three months earlier but still felt as though the events were happening fresh before her eyes.

Although she and Randy had parted on civil terms, she could not believe her marriage of 25 years was over. Like so many women, she had thought she would be married to the same man forever. So when he told her he was leaving her for another woman, she was stunned and shocked on such a deep level that she thought she might actually crumble apart.

Finola's two best friends were also divorced women, and she had promised herself she would not become cold and bitter as they had. But she could feel the bitterness, anger, fear, doubt, and resentment insinuate themselves into her very bones, for now she was alone and it had been a long time since she had been on her own.

She had many things to think about, worry about, and become depressed about, including her financial situation, which was hanging by a thread. She had her full-time job, her two children were grown and fairly independent, and Randy had agreed to alimony, although it made Finola feel ashamed to have to continue letting him pay her way through life. But she needed every penny if she wanted to keep a roof over her head.

The emotional emptiness was another story. Even though she and Randy had been growing apart for several years, she still felt as though his departure had torn a huge hole in her spirit. Walking around the home they had made together, she felt like a ghost, not really present in her own life.

Finola's sister, Jeannie, tried to convince her she was still an attractive woman with much to offer a man, but Finola was determined not to jump back into the dating pool. Something urged her to take advantage of the solitude that was thrust upon her. Finola began to spend more time rediscovering some of the passions she had given up long ago when pleasing her husband had become her top priority. She took up gardening, spent more time reading, and began attending local political meetings.

As the weeks passed, Finola noticed something new. When she woke up in the morning, she looked forward to getting out of bed. In fact, she was excited to get out of bed! As alone as she sometimes felt, she also felt the thrill of independence and of finally owning her own life and her own time. She decided to fill her hours solely with the things she loved: friends, her children, her garden, and her passions, new and old. There were many things in which she wanted to get involved now that she was responsible only for herself, and she signed up for classes at the local college.

> **You shall be a crown of beauty in the hand of the Lord, and a royal diadem in the hand of your God.**
>
> **Isaiah 62:3**

There she met Jeff, a professor who was also divorced. They began dating, but Finola made a promise that she would never lose herself to a man again. From now on, she came first, and her dreams took top priority. She didn't know if anything was to come of her new relationship. But she did know she had survived her divorce and was now on her way to living a fuller, happier life.

Up from the Ashes

God, raise my body and my spirit up
from the ashes and let me float for a
while amongst the angels. Take my hand
and lead me from the depths of
dark thoughts to a joyful new perspective.
Gently direct me to greater heights of
happiness. I cannot do this alone, God,
so be my chaperone as I strive to become
a better person. Help me rise
to each and every occasion and shine
a little brighter every day.

130
pg 132
141
156
137-138
147

CHAPTER 4

The Blessing of Conflict

Surround me with your presence, Lord, in this time of stress. You are the rock to which I cling when I am weak and weary. You are able to soothe and comfort as well as strengthen me. Help me to be a voice of reason in times of chaos. Firm up my convictions. Keep me stable and help me to make right choices. Let me absorb your love so I can once again face the world with a steady mind and heart.

An Angel to Guide Me

Lord, send me an angel to stand before me and clear a way through this conflict. Send me a companion to talk with me and walk with me through the long, dark night. Send me a sage to teach me the ways of the world and keep me centered in spirit. Lord, send me an angel to lift me up on gossamer wings of hope and love and faith. Amen.

From the depths of despair, the seed of joy is planted. From the ashes of destruction, the foundation of hope is erected. From the chaos of conflict, the song of peace is composed.

Outside the Comfort Zone

The worst time of Beth's life was when she and her coworkers went on strike. Long afterward she continued to have nightmares about it. Striking was the last thing she wanted to do. Her husband had a good job, and she was working just because she wanted to. She really didn't see any need to strike for higher wages or better conditions. Besides that, her religious beliefs conflicted with the confrontational nature of a strike.

But pressure from colleagues made striking almost mandatory for Beth. Coworkers pointed out that others weren't as fortunate as she was. They desperately needed their income. Beth, they reasoned, was obligated to join in support of her friends.

Still reluctant, Beth, a meek person by nature, sought counsel from her pastor, but he chose to remain neutral. Her husband, himself a union member, advised her to strike, fearing that Beth might become the object of reprisals and her friends might turn on her and make life unpleasant if she refused to go along. So, against her instincts and better judgment, she joined the strikers.

In a large company, the issues aren't so personal, but she worked for a close-knit, community-based business. Every action produced a reaction. Feelings were hurt. Strikers and nonstrikers became adversaries. They lost trust in their supervisors with whom they had enjoyed good working relationships. It was like a bad dream.

On the first day of picketing, they walked up and down the sidewalk until Beth's hip began to hurt. Some folks came to cheer them on, but people they thought were friends and supporters jeered at them. Beth was crushed.

Beth was assigned the job of monitoring the shortwave radio. She turned to the frequency to receive messages from their union leaders, and management cut into their broadcast with a blaring version of the song "We've Only Just Begun." Chills ran up and down her spine to hear the implicit threat, realizing the bosses knew every move they were making because there were spies in the union organization.

After weeks of dirty tricks and distasteful activities, the strike was finally settled. But for Beth, each day had been agony. She felt her self-esteem was damaged. In her husband's labor union, strikes were just a big game, with posturing on both sides. When the strike was over, everything was forgotten and life went on as usual. Not in Beth's case.

The day the workers went back to their jobs, her supervisor called her into the office. The supervisor was angry because she had promised management the full support of her department. The woman thought the workers had let her down and pledged never to forget or forgive what they had done to her. She grilled Beth for two hours, during which time Beth's post stood empty and unproductive.

Finally Beth, who prized peace and compromise above confrontation, made the decision to speak out. If there was to be any value to this great sacrifice she had made to her personal integrity, she felt she had to respond to her supervisor's heavy-handed tactics that had caused the workers to suffer even before the strike.

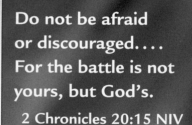

Do not be afraid or discouraged.... For the battle is not yours, but God's.

2 Chronicles 20:15 NIV

Saying a prayer for help, Beth stepped out of her usual quiet role to challenge the supervisor.

She didn't know exactly what came over her but felt it must have been a nudge from the Lord. Beth told the boss the workers were disappointed in her. They thought that because the woman had once been a union leader and had only recently been promoted to management she should have known how the workers felt and supported them.

Beth wondered if she was just being naive by assuming people in authority should care about their workers and not just themselves. Quietly, Beth asserted herself and let her boss know that she was prepared to stand up for fair treatment and respect for *all* workers.

She had stepped out of her comfort zone. At the time, it felt like the end of the world to Beth. Years passed before many work relationships were repaired. But because of Beth's pronouncements, her boss came to grudgingly respect her, and Beth gained a new sense of self-respect and empowerment. Maybe that wasn't such a bad trade.

Our Strength Is My Song

Father, your weakness is stronger than the strength of the weakest man. Since I first sang "Jesus Loves Me" at age 3, I have known of your power. I may be weak, but you are strong. Your strength has been my song. But through the years my song has weakened. In this present crisis, I need your assurance that you are still there, that you will stand by me, that I can still lean on you. O Lord, break through this wall of doubt and weakness and strengthen me for the trials ahead.

"Why me?" Have you ever uttered those words when you were up to your ears in trouble? But why *not* you?

Paul, Timothy, and other apostles were continually in trouble and in conflict with the authorities for spreading the gospel. They endured humiliation, punishment, imprisonment, and even risked death many times. Jesus himself bore the hostility of his contemporaries and gave up his life for us. So why not you and me? Paul reminds us that we are not to lose heart when we are punished, "for the Lord disciplines those whom he loves" (Hebrews 12:6). Further, we are to endure trials for the sake of discipline, which yields righteousness and healing. Healing is one of the blessings born of struggle and conflict.

*F*ear is my enemy, Lord. Fear weakens
me and makes me see trouble even when
there is none. But you have taught me
that fear is a sign of a lack of faith and
that I needn't be afraid when you are
near. Strengthen my faith, Father, and give
me courage. Help me to live fearlessly.
With you at my side, who or what can
harm me? Amen.

*T*here are times in everyone's life when
something constructive is born out of
adversity…when things seem so bad
that you've got to grab your fate by the
shoulders and shake it.

AUTHOR UNKNOWN

We also boast in our sufferings,
knowing that suffering produces
endurance, and endurance produces
character, and character produces
hope, and hope does not disappoint
us, because God's love has been
poured into our hearts through the
Holy Spirit that has been given to us.

Romans 5:3–5

*I*f you avoid trouble,
   Here's a word to the wise:
   Blessings often come dressed
   In trouble's disguise.

Can Do!

Adah, who had reached the venerable age of 96, regarded growing old as one of the greatest struggles in life. The process had happened gradually, but with each new deterioration of her body and mind, panic had hit. It hurt her to know she couldn't do the things she once did easily.

She became lame, forgetful, and easily confused. Her eyesight dimmed, making pastimes like puzzles, craftwork, and reading difficult to do. She lost so much of her hearing that she misunderstood others or she missed out on conversations entirely. Such miscommunications sometimes made people think she was losing her mind.

She became frustrated when others had to do things for her. She felt like a prisoner in her own body, a hostage to the aging process.

But Adah refused to give up. She worked to keep up her spirits so as not to get down on herself and think she was useless. She tried to get out regularly. She always went to church on Sunday. Listening to sermons and singing the familiar hymns gave her a boost, even though she thought her voice sounded like an old rusty gate. She liked to meet other people, talk and hear the news, and learn their problems, which were usually worse than hers. She also attended a sewing circle and a seniors' group, and she went out to lunch whenever she could wrangle an invitation.

Her best spirit-lifter was crocheting. Adah enjoyed watching the colors of yarn blend and the pattern grow. She would think about the person who was going to receive the gift and say a prayer for him or her. Then she would imagine their pleasure at receiving the afghan, or pillow, or cuddly animal. When her mind was on her craftwork project, she didn't think too much about herself, and it felt so good to accomplish something.

Her daughter was planning the annual vacation for the whole family, which included four generations. It would be exhilarating to see everyone and experience new and different things. At these times, Adah felt young and like one of the crowd again. She could still go fishing or boating, take rides in the country to see scenery and wildlife, and eat out a lot. At the end of the week, there was usually a fish fry, followed by roasting marshmallows over a campfire. She wondered how many 96-year-olds got to do that.

Adah recognized the blessings in growing old. For one, she wasn't a slave to the alarm clock anymore. She liked to get up at a reasonable hour but didn't have to. Second, she no longer had to prove herself. She'd done all the things she was likely to accomplish in her lifetime. Third, she could nap whenever she liked without feeling guilty. Best of all, no one expected her to be of help, and when she did help, it was rewarding to know she was still able to do so.

She realized the Lord had been good to her. Adah felt blessed to have a home, someone to care for her, three good meals a day, a place to sleep, and things to do. Her grandchildren and great-grandchildren lived nearby and stopped in now and then. They all played games like dominoes or tossing a ball. On her 96th birthday, she even played musical chairs.

People did helpful and comforting things for her, but they didn't fuss over her and presume she couldn't do anything for herself. They treated her like a grown-up. Adah liked that.

One of her favorite Bible verses, which her daughter called her "can-do" verse, was Philippians 4:13: "I can do all things through him who strengthens me." Adah intended to do things for herself as long as she could and not to mourn over the things she couldn't do. Her motto was: Concentrate on the things you *can* do and be thankful to God for them.

Ever at My Side

Father, you have been at my side
throughout the decades of my life.
It has not always been easy to face
the world in my diminished capacity,
yet through the good times and the
bad, your love has brought serenity
and beauty to all my days. I collect the
moments and hours beyond counting
and lay them at your feet as a bouquet.
You have honored my life, and
in response I honor you with my
determination to live fully and to
continue serving you to the
end of my days.

*G*od acknowledges that he sends both blessings and curses: "See, I am setting before you today a blessing and a curse" (Deuteronomy 11:26). God sends blessings to those people who obey his commandments and curses to those who do not. He wants us to give him our hearts and our souls. He wants our complete obedience. Being human, we tend to make mistakes in judgment, and before long we find ourselves in trouble. But trouble doesn't need to be permanent. God gives us

> I consider that the sufferings of this present time are not worth comparing with the glory about to be revealed to us. For the creation waits with eager longing for the revealing of the children of God.
>
> **Romans 8:18–19**

ways to work through our struggles. We can pray; we can humble ourselves before him; we can ask for his presence and strength. God does not promise to keep us out of trouble, but he does promise to be there for us and to bless us when we obey.

You have given us the gift of prayer, Lord. Sometimes my words flow easily, but other times it is difficult to pray. When I come to you, help me to state what is in my heart.

You have promised to be near to all who call upon you, Lord. I ask you to be with me now, to hear this and all my prayers, and to teach me to pray properly. Let me learn to carry all my joys and sorrows, triumphs and failures to you, knowing you will celebrate with me in the good times, share with me in times of conflict, and help me find solutions. Amen.

O God, Our Help in Ages Past

O God, our help in ages past,
Our hope for years to come,
Our shelter from the stormy blast,
And our eternal home.

Under the shadow of thy throne
Thy saints have dwelt secure;
Sufficient is thine arm alone,
And our defense is sure.

Before the hills in order stood
Or earth received her frame,
From everlasting thou art God,
To endless years the same.

ISAAC WATTS

In Fear's Grip

It was a routine annual visit to the doctor's office for Claire's husband, Max. He had the checkup and blood test and came home with a good appetite for lunch. A few days later, his internist called to report the results of the blood test.

"Everything's fine," he said, "except your PSA reading for your prostate is a bit high." The doctor went on to say that it was likely a common benign condition, but he would schedule an appointment with an oncologist for tests just as a precaution.

Two weeks later, Max returned from the specialist's office with shoulders drooping. This time he wasn't hungry. In answer to Claire's questioning look, he whispered in disbelief, "I have cancer." They held each other and cried. Then they prayed.

From that day on, their lives changed drastically. Fear moved in with them, and they felt its chilling presence constantly. Cancer was a disease that happened to someone else, not to a healthy, muscular building tradesman like Max, who always volunteered to drive others to the hospital for their treatments. In fact, he was in the process of driving a friend downtown twice a week to visit her ailing husband. The irony of it made the ache in their hearts even greater.

"Lord, we know you are with us," they prayed, "but we're so scared." Yet there was more to come.

"Let's take a few more tests just to make sure there's nothing else hiding in there," the oncologist suggested later. Their anxiety grew as weeks went by before they received the results. Four suspicious shadows showed up on the MRI.

"They could be harmless cysts," the doctor commented. As it turned out, three of them were cysts, but the fourth shadow in the kidney was not. Now Max had two separate cancers to deal with. The fear intensified and became even more unbearable.

Max and Claire decided they needed a strategy to fight both the cancer and the fear. Max wanted to be a survivor, not a victim. First, they needed to find a kidney specialist to remove the diseased organ. They wanted to get the best surgeon they could for the job.

One of the first blessings came when their internist tracked down the head of the nephrology department at a prestigious teaching hospital for a recommendation. It turned out that one of the school's best was practicing at their own hospital. Dr. Kay was a young man who treated the couple like his own parents. He was upbeat, confident, and experienced—the best transplant surgeon the city had to offer. Little by little, fear began to lose its grip on them.

Another blessing occurred when their daughter, a nurse, suggested they learn all they could about the disease so they could be a part of the treatment. Max and Claire read books, talked to other patients, and checked with friends and family in the medical profession. One of the most important things they learned was that cancer isn't necessarily fatal. Many options existed that weren't available in the past. They also learned by experience that diagnosis is not an exact science and that doctors don't always agree, making it wise to seek second opinions.

A third blessing happened as the couple drew closer together to comfort each other. Claire assured Max, "Whatever happens to you, happens to me." She became his advocate, going to every appointment, asking questions, arguing, and making sure he was getting the best treatment possible.

They refused to wallow in self-pity. Taking a tip from writer Norman Cousins, they avoided sad and sentimental music, books, and movies and pursued humor and laughter. They sought the company of other people who had gone through similar crises and survived. They leaned on friends and family to help them and to keep their spirits high. They kept busy with activities to distract them.

Finally, they learned to pray more. Often during her prayers, Claire could actually feel the presence of God assuring her and leading her forward.

Their spirits began to rise as Dr. Kay laid out all the options. Max chose to have the surgery first to remove the kidney, then radiation later for the prostate cancer.

On the day of surgery, ten friends arrived with their pastor to form a circle of prayer in the hospital waiting room. Another fellow, a young member of their church and an employee of the hospital, rolled up to the door on his inline skates to wish them well. The sight of him on rollerblades brought laughter and a release of tension. At that moment, Claire knew the surgery and radiation would be successful.

Max has now reached his eighth year of being cancer free. Each year past the date, the couple's fear lessened. They have learned to breathe a little easier. Though Max and Claire wouldn't have chosen to go through that ordeal, they felt they had gained both courage and strength by staring fear in the face and, with God's help, conquering it.

Part of the Plan

Father, my world that was so orderly is
now falling apart. How can it be?
I have loved you and followed your laws;
I have tried to live according to your
word. How could things go wrong?
I don't understand what is happening.
I know your ways are higher than my
ways, and your thoughts are higher than
my thoughts. Lord, please give me the
wisdom to comprehend. Help me to see
this is all part of your plan to give me
a future with hope.

God is our refuge and strength,
a very present help in trouble.
Therefore, we will not fear, though
the earth should change, though
the mountains shake in the heart
of the sea; though its waters roar
and foam, though the mountains
tremble with its tumult.

Psalm 46:1–3

Conflicts can occur in many areas of our lives. We may have personal conflicts, work conflicts, health conflicts, and more. Even the slightest conflict can plunge us deep into turmoil. We become tense, restless, distracted. We often cannot sleep until the issues that unsettle us are resolved or until we feel healed and safe. We must remember that God offers us peace and "refuge under the shelter of [his] wings" (Psalm 61:4). When conflicts of any kind rob us of peace, we can turn to God for refuge and resolution.

For a Friend

God of healing and compassion,
please hear me now as I ask for healing
of a beloved friend. Ease his pain and
help him to feel the love of his family
and friends and, most of all, your love,
God. You made my friend. You numbered
the hairs on his head. He is your child,
and you alone know his needs. Father,
surround him with your peace and
calm his anxiety. Let him know with
your tender touch that healing is
his for the asking. Amen.

Motivating Factor

When Jenny retired, friends asked if she could think of one experience that contributed most to her career as a teacher. After a slight hesitation, she said, "A case of double pneumonia when I was 13 years old."

Her colleagues stared in surprise at this multitalented woman who was poised to begin a new job and a new career the week following retirement.

"Yes, it's true," Jenny continued. "I was very ill and nearly died. Only the prayers of family and friends pulled me through. My hospital stay and convalescence were long."

She explained that antibiotics had not yet been introduced to the public, and it wasn't until the following year that sulfa and penicillin were used on the battlefield in World War II, so her recovery took five months.

Jenny had kept up with her schoolwork during her convalescence, but her family moved just before the school year ended. The officials at the new school had no record of her work and refused to promote her. Jenny felt hurt and humiliated. Bright and hard-working, she did not understand why she should have to repeat the seventh grade.

"I was kind of rusty in math," Jenny recalled, "so I asked the new teacher a question about division of fractions. She brushed me aside, saying, 'Never mind; you're not going to pass anyway.' That small cruelty was a turning point in my life. After that, I felt numb.

"I brooded all through the summer. I couldn't eat or sleep. The days passed in a fog. I had lost all hope. As I look back on it now, I can see that I was in a deep depression. By the time fall rolled around, I knew I had to do something. Each time a classmate taunted me about being held back, all I could think of was 'I'll show them!'"

> For surely I know the plans I have for you, says the Lord, plans for your welfare and not for harm, to give you a future with hope.
>
> Jeremiah 29:11

That motivation caused Jenny to campaign to be restored to her rightful grade level and to graduate with her class. Then, in high school, she worked doubly hard to achieve a straight-A average, again to prove herself. Once she reached the rank of valedictorian of her class in the city's largest high school, Jenny was tempted to sit back and relax. "By that time, though, those good study habits were ingrained," Jenny said. "Besides, with my blue-collar background and the fact that my grandfather had been illiterate, I made my parents terribly proud. I wanted to keep on making them happy."

Another incident at the beginning of her final year in high school made Jenny more determined than ever to excel. At a meeting of the senior class, a counselor was showing off. With the scores of standardized tests in front of him, he claimed he could correctly predict a student's grade-point average.

One of Jenny's friends called out her name. Because she was quiet and modest, the counselor didn't know her. He looked up her scores and pronounced that she was probably no more than a B student. Jenny's classmates howled and quickly let the counselor know he was looking at a straight-A student. The counselor blushed and labeled Jenny an "overachiever."

Jenny had laughed, not caring what he called her. She knew her grades had landed her a high-paying summer job and a scholarship offer from a Big Ten university. Those connections led to more opportunities, and her hard work and prayers did the rest.

She admits it was difficult living through the year of her illness and recuperation. The setbacks were a terrible blow to her adolescent psyche. The experience taught her how fragile the teenage ego is and how carefully teachers need to nurture children. It completely changed her perception of the way students should be treated. It influenced her entire teaching career.

At the time, Jenny had thought it was the blackest period of her life, but she sees it differently now. That series of events made her strong. She had been a good student in school but not great. She was shy, self-conscious, and industrious, but a bit of an underachiever. Her struggle with her ordeal changed all that.

"I believe God sent that illness to motivate me and make me more determined," Jenny concluded. "He's been with me ever since, to push me ahead and grant me fulfillment in my work with children. And now, years later, at my retirement, I'm getting the chance to follow my 'road not taken,' a new career in the arts. The blessings are still coming."

The apostle Paul was imprisoned for spreading the gospel of Christ. Corrie ten Boom, a young Dutch woman, was interned in Nazi concentration camps for aiding Jews during World War II. Centuries apart, at different times in history, both were able to transcend the humiliation and brutality of their environment. Determined to conquer their circumstances, they refused to allow bitterness and hatred into their hearts. Clinging to the knowledge of God's love, they prayed, sang hymns, and helped others

> Indeed we call blessed those who showed endurance. You have heard of the endurance of Job, and you have seen the purpose of the Lord, how the Lord is compassionate and merciful.
>
> **James 5:11**

through the ordeal. These two believers learned that no matter how difficult the conditions or how strong the enemy, God is stronger still. In the words of Paul, "We are more than conquerors through him who loved us" (Romans 8:37).

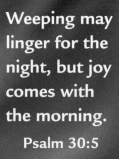

*L*ord, sometimes the needs of my family and friends come at me from all sides. These demands create a conflict of my time and attention. It is difficult to sort them out and respond to them all fairly. Please answer my call. Help me to shoulder my burdens. Show me how to discern which problems most need my attention and which I can entrust to you. Lord, help me find the answer and peace.

Weeping may linger for the night, but joy comes with the morning.
Psalm 30:5

You Are the Shepherd

Lord, you are the shepherd who leads us
beside still waters so we may be restored.
Only you can comfort us. You bring us
blessings even in the midst of trouble
when we draw closer to you and commit
our cause to you. You alone have the
power to change lives. Pour out your
strength on us in our conflict and heal us.
Amen.

*H*ow often we look upon God as our last…resource! We go to him because we have nowhere else to go. And then we learn that the storms of life have driven us, not upon the rocks, but into the desired haven.

GEORGE MACDONALD

CHAPTER 5

Dawn of a New Day

Guide Me Gently

Lord, guide me gently into the light of a new day filled with hope and joyful expectancy. Take my hand and walk beside me, making my path straight and my troubles few and far between. Keep my eyes looking toward the sun and let the darkness of past mistakes fade away behind me. Lord, lead me into a new life filled with your abundant good grace and your glorious presence. Amen.

*P*raised be my Lord and God, with all His creatures, and especially our brother the sun, who brings us the day and brings us the light; fair is he, and he shines with great splendor. O Lord, he is a sign to us of you! Praised be my Lord for our sister the moon, and for stars, set clear and lovely in the heaven.

St. Francis of Assisi

*T*he greatest gift of time is that with each moment it brings a precious new opportunity to be renewed in body, mind, and spirit. Time bestows the blessing of another day and another chance to live the life of our dreams.

Becoming

Lucille felt that her life was over. She had been married for 30 years to her high school sweetheart, and now he was gone. The cancer that took Andy from her had moved through his body with such speed she was certain it was a living, breathing demon. He had once been a vibrant man, full of passion for life. She simply could not grasp that he would no longer be there every morning, jumping out of bed, eager to greet the new day with the energy of men half his age.

> **Then your light shall break forth like the dawn, and your healing shall spring up quickly; your vindicator shall go before you, the glory of the Lord shall be your rear guard.**
>
> Isaiah 58:8

The cancer had begun in his colon and then spread before surgery could stop it. Andy had somehow come to terms with his fate, and in their last days together, he had been the sensible one, at peace with what was happening. For Lucille, it was nothing but chaos. He had been her everything from the moment they met and fell in love. They had married and raised two lovely daughters. He had been her life, her reason for being in the world.

Now the house echoed her deep loneliness. She could still feel Andy's palpable presence throughout the rooms he had helped her design. She grieved in silence, sometimes in the presence of their daughters, sometimes with friends, but mostly alone. When alone, she could cry and moan without embarrassment. Then she could call out to Andy to come back to her, and she could curse God for taking him.

As the weeks went by, her bouts with grief subsided and Lucille felt numb and depressed. She was grateful for the loving care of friends and family members, but she found herself wanting to be alone at times. Only something was different. Before, she wanted to be alone so she could grieve in private. Now, she wanted to be alone so she could do something she hadn't done in years, something Andy had always urged her to get more involved in, but she had always claimed she didn't have the time or energy for it.

In truth, she'd had plenty of time and energy. What she hadn't had was courage—the courage to paint. As a young woman, Lucille had loved painting, and it was one of the things that had attracted Andy to her. He loved her artistic, fiery spirit and her creativity and imagination. As she had grown older and become busy raising a family, she'd relegated the paints to a back room and then to a closet.

Now there was no more family to raise and no more Andy to dote over and do things with. Lucille found herself more and more drawn to that closet and the paint supplies. One day, she actually took out the supplies. Two days later, she got the courage to open the paints. Three days after that, she pulled out a large blank canvas and set up the old easel.

Little by little, Lucille edged closer to the painting she had long ago deserted. On the day she actually stroked the paint on the canvas, she felt such a rush of pleasure and sheer joy that she turned around, sure she would see Andy standing there beaming at her. He wasn't there physically, but Lucille was sure he was there in spirit, urging her onward. "Paint!" she could hear him say in his enthused voice, "Paint and be happy!"

Lucille's heart still ached every day for her beloved husband. But now she was certain her life was not over and she could go on and find joy again, even as she dreamed of one day joining Andy in heaven.

Painting gave her that joy. She felt as though she was rediscovering herself with each stroke. When she finished a painting, she no longer waited for ages before trying another. Lucille painted outdoors every day, which inspired her to take up another long-lost hobby: gardening. Always, no matter what she did, she felt Andy at her side.

She was falling in love with life again. She was becoming Lucille all over again, and that, she knew, was what Andy would have wanted for her.

*B*linded by pain and sadness, our human eyes often miss the spark of light that dances upon the far horizon. Our vision narrowed by fear, we sometimes don't see the rainbow forming just at the edges of those dreadfully gray clouds. With a simple change of perspective, what looked bleak now reveals the seed of newfound joy. With an open heart and mind, the sufferings of yesterday now become the strength, courage, and kindness we need to make a beautiful tomorrow for ourselves and for all we meet.

I Rise

God of my heart, teach me to rise again
from the depths of suffering. Things
have been so bleak and tough lately, but
I know there is always a reason to be
hopeful, and my heart refuses to give
up and give in. Give me the power to
spread my wings and soar once again
with renewed spirit and a freshness of
mind and with courage to face whatever
challenges befall me. Help me to be
an example to others in need of
hope and a pair of strong wings to those
too weak to fly. Amen.

*L*ife operates in cycles of darkness and light, of cold and warmth, of death and new growth. Nothing remains stagnant forever, and the potential for joy always exists side by side with suffering.

*T*here are times, Lord, when I feel as though I cannot bear to make it through the night. This is one of those times. The darkness and despair is overwhelming, and I fear I do not have the strength and patience to wait out the dawn. Help me to be strong. Give me courage so that I can handle whatever comes my way this night and rise tomorrow with a newfound faith and a joyful expectation. So let it be.

Wingspan

I feel like a bird with a broken wing,
unable to take flight and soar above my
problems and challenges without your
loving mercy and gentle, caring guidance.
With you beside me, Lord, I know that
with patience and determination
I can strengthen what is broken within
me and spread my spirit to its full
wingspan. I can once again fly high and
free above the worries of the earth below
and meet you face to face among the
glorious clear skies. Amen.

The Weight

When Margot stepped on the scale, she held her breath. It took almost a full minute before she had the courage to open her eyes and look at the numbers on the digital readout. The sad fact was that when she did open her eyes to look she couldn't see the scale without bending over.

The number staring back at her made her knees go weak. *How did I let this happen?* she thought. *How did I let my weight creep up so high?* She broke down and cried.

Margot couldn't remember ever being thin, but there was a time when she was lean and healthy. At five feet four inches, she had once hovered around 150 pounds, most of it muscle. But now her small frame bore the weight of 280 pounds and most of it was fat. It had happened in just a few years.

The weight of her shame was worse. She no longer did things she once enjoyed, like playing tennis, swimming (she wouldn't be caught dead in a swimsuit!), or going out at night with friends. It was just too hard to find something to wear that didn't make her look or feel like a walking tent.

She had tried many crash diets, and the weight would come off, then creep back on, usually more than before. Like many women, Margot would have tried anything to be slim and sexy. But now, looking at herself and knowing she was closing in on 300 pounds, she felt defeated. She wanted nothing more than to disappear.

Margot walked into the bedroom and sat on the bed. She was fully aware of the heaviness of every pound of flesh she carried, added to the weight of her feelings of self-loathing. She closed her eyes and sat quietly, trying to find some semblance of strength within her to change her life.

But she could find nothing. Her faith had not been rewarded in the past, and she was certain it wouldn't be now, so why bother? That night, she decided she was destined to be fat, ugly, and unworthy, and she ate more food in one hour than she used to consume in a day. It was as if she had given up on herself and on God.

Sitting at the dinner table, Margot felt sorry for herself for the zillionth time. The TV was on, and a home-shopping program was featuring beautiful plus-size models and actresses. Margot watched with distaste. *Who do they think they're kidding?* she thought. *They would all kill to be thin.* But the longer she watched, the more she realized these women were not dying to be thin. In fact, they were living it up big time, and they were happy!

In a flash of understanding, Margot realized she would never lose the weight until she could first accept herself just the way she was. It was like a riddle: You won't be happy later unless you can be happy now. She began to smile, feeling for the first time in a long time like she actually could do this. She could take better care of herself, get help, get healthy, and lose weight. More important, however, she could do something right now to start.

Margot stepped into the bathroom and looked straight at her reflection. Without flinching, she spoke the words out loud, "You are perfect just the way you are, and I love you." At first it felt silly, but she kept on saying the words

> **No testing has overtaken you that is not common to everyone. God is faithful, and he will not let you be tested beyond your strength, but with the testing he will also provide the way out so that you may be able to endure it.**
>
> **1 Corinthians 10:13**

until they began to feel natural and empowering. When she was done, she noticed a change in her posture. She was standing taller, more assured.

The next morning, Margot enrolled in an exercise class for overweight women and spoke with a nutritional counselor about a food plan. It would be a very long road, but this time Margot had a secret weapon. With the Lord's strength and help, she would do it for herself. And she had the newfound belief and enthusiasm of knowing that even if she only lost ten pounds, she was still one heck of a woman just the way she was.

*H*ope is like a kite with a long tail of sturdy string that even the most downcast of us can manage to grab onto. No matter how bleak our lives may appear to be, no matter how flat on our backs our troubles have pushed us, we can still reach up and take the kite string of hope in our hand, and it will carry us aloft into a new and brighter day. And if we haven't enough strength left within us to hold on tight, God will step in and do for us what we cannot do alone. God's strength will keep us flying and soaring, higher and higher, until we touch the heavens.

A Fresh Start

Thank you for this new day, Lord, and for
this chance to start fresh. Things have
not been good lately, but you have given
me the faith to keep looking forward.
For your love, for your mercy, and for
your grace, I give thanks. With you I can
accomplish great things that I never could
without you. You have restored my hope
and made my life brand-new. Amen.

God, give me strength to get through this day. Give me hope to rise anew tomorrow with the courage to go forth and do what needs to be done. Give me a little joy here and there to remind me that the situation is not as bad as it seems. Give me laughter when my heart is heavy. Give me understanding when my mind is filled with confusion. But most of all, give me one more day to get it right. Thank you, God.

A New Day Is Here

Today is a new day,
　　And I am ready to face it with
　　　courage.
　　Today is a new chance,
　　And I am ready to live with
　　　conviction.
　　Today is a new opportunity,
　　And I am ready to make better
　　　choices.
　　Today is a new possibility,
　　And I am ready to face any obstacle.
　　Today is a new way of thinking,
　　Of walking and being and doing.
　　Today is a new day,
　　And I am ready to live every
　　　moment.

To Breathe Again

Macy was a single mother with two young children and an ex-husband who didn't know the meaning of "child support." She didn't really like working ten-hour days as an advertising executive and leaving her children at the day-care center on the first floor of her office building. But she made a good living and could see no other way to support her family.

When the pink slip appeared on her desk, Macy was shocked. It made her feel sick to think her boss didn't even have the courage to tell her face to face. Then she learned her boss had been the first one to get a pink slip. Apparently, the owner of the company was bringing in his son and other family members to run the ship. Nepotism had won out over loyalty, experience, and skill.

> By awesome deeds you answer us with deliverance, O God of our salvation; you are the hope of all the ends of the earth and of the farthest seas.
>
> **Psalm 65:5**

Utter panic came over her, and Macy felt as though she could not breathe. She was to leave that day with a severance package equal to exactly one month's salary. After ten years with the company, this was all they thought she was worth.

Driving home that afternoon, Macy felt numb and scared. She had no idea what her future would hold or how she would take care of her children. She looked back at her two young toddlers, both asleep in their car seats, and longed to be able to stay at home and spend more time with them, just being their mom.

That night, Macy lay awake for hours as she went over how far her savings would take them. She had her 401k but did not want to break into that; she had hoped to roll it over to another retirement plan. With her regular savings and her severance pay, she realized she had barely two months' worth of living expenses. She had to find a new job and decent day care in the next two months. She would need to begin hunting the next day.

Later that night, one of her sons came into her room and crawled into bed. He was hot with fever. Before long, Macy had both boys in bed with her. Both were sick, and she did her best to tend to them. As she finally snuggled in to sleep, she lay with each boy on either side of her sleeping soundly. It broke her heart to think she was missing so much of their lives because of having to work to keep a roof over their heads. How could she, though, make a living and make a life? She said a quiet prayer for guidance, asking for a sign or a clue pointing to what she should do next.

When morning came, Macy awakened first. The boys were still sleeping, and thankfully their fevers had gone down. Quietly Macy got up. She opened the front door and grabbed the newspaper, carrying it to the kitchen table where she plopped it down. When it landed, one of the sections slipped off the table and onto the floor. It was the business section, and on its front page was an article about the growing need for consultants in various industries. Macy forgot all about the brewing coffee and read the article twice with a growing sense of excitement.

Being a consultant was a perfect idea and one she could set up quickly with her extensive list of contacts. She could stay at home and work around her boys. The process would be hard, she realized, and the business might not take off right away. But Macy felt certain this was the right path for her. She had prayed for a sign and been given one. She felt like she could breathe again.

The long dark night of the soul always gives way to the dawn of a new day. It is the law of the universe, the cycle of nature and the spirit. No matter how much we suffer or how bleak the world around us appears, the next moment is alive and pulsating with the possibility of healing and renewal. The future carries the promise of happiness restored if we hold on tight and ride out the storm. Hope is the vehicle that delivers us from the depths of despair up to the light again, where we can see ourselves and our lives from a whole new perspective. With hope in our hearts, we rise to greet that new day, stronger and wiser than before.

At Night

O Lord God, who has given us the night
for rest, I pray that in my sleep my soul
may remain awake to you, steadfastly
adhering to your love. As I lay aside
my cares to relax and relieve my mind,
may I not forget your infinite and
unresting care for me. And in this way,
let my conscience be at peace, so that
when I rise tomorrow, I am refreshed
in body, mind and soul.

JOHN CALVIN

*S*ometimes, I think, the things we see
Are shadows of the things to be;
That what we plan we build;
That every hope that hath been
   crossed,
And every dream we thought
   was lost,
In heaven shall be fulfilled.

PHOEBE CARY

*L*et me feel the glory of your redemption and renewal, God, as I embark on this new life. Today I will walk with you to guide me, to direct my every step, knowing that with your love and wisdom, I shall not be misled. Today I will have hope, faith, and courage as I have never had before, knowing that you are always there to give me the strength I need. Amen.

Second Chances

Father, within you is life itself. In your
presence, which permeates all things,
there is the promise of renewal and
the gift of second chances. In your
power, there is the key to finding truth.
In your wisdom, there is the master
plan for achieving any dream. Remove
the boundaries of fear and doubt that
separate me from you and embrace me
fully into your being. Unite my heart
with yours, my mind with yours,
my spirit with yours. Let me be one
with you today.

Wings of Angels

Lift me up on the wings of angels, Lord,
to soar above the clouds where the
skies are clear with infinite possibilities.
Empower me with hope and faith so I
may rise above my challenges and see the
vista spread out before me—a landscape
abundant with opportunities for renewal
and happiness. Let me fly higher than
I ever thought I could, Lord, as I touch
the robes of angels cheering me on
in my flight. Amen.

The Real Thing

Brittany looked down at the tiny pill in the palm of her hand. She knew she had two choices: take the pill and be able to get through the night or don't take the pill and be sleep-deprived and anxious, eventually having one of her panic attacks.

She took the pill. After all, it was just an antianxiety drug prescribed to thousands of people for legitimate reasons. It never crossed her mind that the prescription was not hers; it belonged to her friend, Susan.

Susan was hesitant to give her friend any more pills. She knew Brittany was overusing them and wondered if Brittany was becoming addicted. Susan could see a change in her friend's behavior. She noticed her becoming more and more negative and always complaining of being run-down and tired. Susan had originally given Brittany the pills after Brittany's mom died, when her friend needed help sleeping and relaxing.

But now Susan felt she had to put her foot down. She informed Brittany that she would not refill the prescription because Brittany was misusing the medication. She advised her to seek help via therapy or counseling.

Brittany refused to believe that her friend was trying to help her. She lashed out at Susan. Brittany went to her own doctor and got a prescription rather than take Susan's advice. She was hurting from her mother's death, and she refused to face it, instead popping a pill to numb the pain.

Still, the pills could only do so much, and before long Brittany was chasing them with alcohol most nights and passing out. It was the only way she knew to keep the pain at bay. It was the only way she knew to survive.

When she was fired from her job for not showing up two days in a row, Brittany lashed out at her boss instead of accepting the blame and the responsibility. She sank deeper into a pill-induced depression and began to shut out the world, only venturing out to buy a bottle of wine or get her pills refilled.

Two weeks had gone by before Brittany realized she was running out of money. She had no savings and now no paycheck. Her solution was to pop a pill and sleep it off, but when she awoke in the middle of the night, the panic and despair were waiting to suffocate her even before she could take another pill to ward it off.

For what seemed like hours, Brittany suffered a panic attack unlike any she had ever had as all her terrors came to the surface, and she cried and trembled in the dark loneliness of her room. Then she recalled a gentle voice talking to her, and she recognized the voice even in the midst of her agony. It was her mother speaking to her a few days before she had passed away. She had told Brittany that she loved her and that everything would be all right.

The memory of that moment made Brittany weep, releasing the pent-up grief and mourning she had never allowed herself to feel. It came out in wave after wave of unbearable sadness. As the night gave way to the first blush of dawn, Brittany began to feel as if she was aware of herself again. It wasn't necessarily a good feeling, but it was empowering, as if she had just rounded a corner and was about to come upon something good.

Brittany spent that day alone, but not because she was miserable. Rather, she spent the day in silent prayer and communion with God, and thinking of her dear mother. She let herself feel whatever emotion surfaced and fully gave herself over to her grief, knowing it was the real feeling and not some pill-created illusion.

It hurt her and scared her, but it was real. It was her life, and now she felt strong enough to face it without the help of a little pill.

*H*eavenly Father, I am like a boat out on the rough waters, searching for the beacon of hope that will guide me back to the safety of the shore. Let your light show me the way home safe and sound. Let your love lead me back to the security of living your will instead of always trying to make my life the way I think it should be. Let your strength be the anchor that keeps me on solid ground and out of danger of the rocks that lurk beneath the waters. Like the majestic lighthouse, bring me back to you, dear God. Amen.

Let Me Be the Guide

Lord, I have made it through the long dark night and now I stand in the joyful light of your love. Help me to spread my wisdom and experience to others so that they, too, may know your grace, your mercy, and your enduring love. Let me be an example to them of how your love heals and renews and makes whole again. Let me be the guide that helps bring others back to the safety of your shores.

No one, including God, ever promised us a life free from struggle and suffering. In fact, we are pretty much assured of challenges and obstacles, for how would we grow and become stronger and more loving without them? How would our character develop without trials that help mold and shape our personality? But what we are promised is that every cloud comes equipped with a silver lining in the form of a powerful and profound life lesson that we will one day be grateful to have learned, no matter how hard the process.

Come the Light

*I*n the darkest hour of night,
I pray for the coming of light,
And with faith alone to guide me,
To continue to do what is right.

In the middle of turmoil and fear,
I pray to keep my senses clear
And move toward the voice calling me
To be healed in God's tender care.

A Promise to Hold Onto

God, I long to be able to say that things are looking up, but right now things are looking down. Really down. I need you more than ever, to help me be strong and capable, because there are others depending on me. I know my suffering won't last forever, even though right now it sure seems that way. But I do believe in you, God, and in your promise of joy and redemption. It is that promise I will hold onto until I once again walk in the light of a new day. Amen.

*L*ord, I thank you for the new day and all its gifts of possibility. I promise to make the best of any situation that comes my way, knowing that with your help I can do anything—all things are possible to those who believe. With gratitude I look forward to a life filled with miracles and blessings of all shapes and sizes. Thank you, Lord, for giving me another chance to truly live.

The Lord, your God, is in your midst, a warrior who gives victory; he will rejoice over you with gladness, he will renew you in his love; he will exult over you with loud singing as on a day of festival.

Zephaniah 3:17–18

I Arise and Go Forth

I arise and go forth into the Dawn of
the New Day, filled with faith and
assurance in the All Good.
I arise, I arise, I sing with joy!
I proclaim the One Life: "In all
and through all."
I arise, I arise, I shout with gladness
that is within me.
I declare this day to be Complete,
Perfect and Eternal.
I respond to Life.

ERNEST HOLMES

CHAPTER 6

The Promise of Prayer

Prayer is the mother and daughter of tears. It is an expiation of sin, a bridge across temptation, a bulwark against affliction. It wipes out conflict, is the work of angels, and is the nourishment of everything spiritual.

ST. JOHN CLIMACUS,
THE LADDER OF DIVINE ASCENT

*L*ord, thank you for the gift of prayer. Help me to begin and end my days in prayer and to weave words of praise and petition through the busy moments of my life. Help me to be aware of the needs of others so I can pray for them. Help me to look honestly at my actions so I can pray for strength in my weakness. And give me patience to sit quietly in your presence, knowing that words have limits and much of your work is accomplished in silence. Amen.

*P*rayer is a great weapon, a rich treasure, a wealth that is never exhausted, an undisturbed refuge, a cause of tranquility, the root of a multitude of blessings, and their source.

ST. JOHN CHRYSOSTOM

A Key

Heavenly Father, mold my prayers
into a key to unlock my confusion.
One minute I think I'm going forward;
the next minute I feel I'm sliding
backward. Yesterday I was filled
with confidence; today I am filled with
doubts. I know you love me, yet I wonder
if you hear me. I long for something,
but I cannot find the words for it.
I know you are my strength and my
salvation, and I put my trust in you
to help me learn to talk with you.
Open my heart to your teachings.
With your help, I will be
a good student.

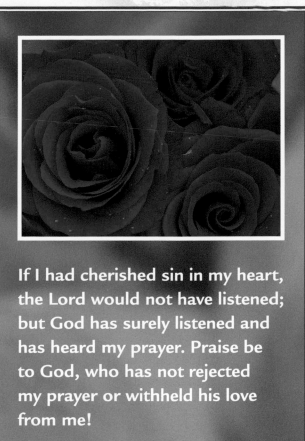

If I had cherished sin in my heart,
the Lord would not have listened;
but God has surely listened and
has heard my prayer. Praise be
to God, who has not rejected
my prayer or withheld his love
from me!

Psalm 66:18–20 NIV

God Is "Unanimous"

On September 11, 2001, Beth was having breakfast with a friend just a mile from the World Trade Center. Her children, seven-year-old Aaron and five-year-old Sophie, were in different schools, miles apart from each other in Manhattan. One minute Beth was buttering a muffin, and the next minute she was caught in the iron grip of terror. Outside the restaurant, people ran screaming from a monstrous cloud of dust and debris. She made her way to the curb, yelling, "Taxi! Taxi!" She had to get her children. The street was a raging river of running people. The world had exploded, and no taxi could take her out of it.

Someone grabbed her arm. "Run!" he cried. "Run!"

She ran the 12 blocks to Aaron's school. The little boy and his classmates were huddled around their teacher. Aaron was pale and trembling. In Beth's arms, he stopped shaking and the color came back to his cheeks. The teacher begged her to stay and help with the other children, but she had to get little Sophie in her school two miles away.

Outside her son's school, Beth stepped into a maelstrom of screaming emergency vehicles, stampeding people, and billowing smoke, with a pervading stench. She was terrified, but Aaron was gripping her hand, trusting her to protect him. She knew she could not do this alone.

She pulled Aaron into a secluded little space beside the school stairs and said, "Look at me, Aaron. We will get Sophie now, and then we will go home. We just need some help." She held both his hands and said, "Pray with me." He nodded solemnly. "God," she said, "We need an angel to help us get Sophie. There, Aaron. Now we have an angel. Everything will be fine."

"I don't see an angel, Mommy," said Aaron.

"But she's here, right in front of us. She doesn't want to be seen, but I can tell she wants us to follow her."

Beth was surprised the little angel story she had spun to comfort Aaron felt more like truth than fantasy. She put her arm around her son and felt confident and protected. The angel steered them around the traffic gridlock, down alleys she never knew existed, and sooner than she believed possible they stood in front of Sophie's school.

Sophie was coloring at her desk, and the teacher had managed to protect her kindergarten class from the chaos outside the school. Beth's heart pounded. How could she tell Sophie that their safe world had exploded into a horror she could not explain? Her daughter would be terrified, and they still had to walk three miles to get home.

She hugged Sophie tightly, and tears ran down her cheeks. Aaron was being very brave, but Sophie would be terrified. She couldn't find one single word to prepare her daughter for the journey home.

Aaron patted his sister's arm. "It's scary outside," he said. "But Mommy prayed for an angel, and she'll walk home with us. We can't see her, but she has really big white wings and a gold halo."

Beth felt that a little bubble of protection surrounded them on the long walk home. Aaron and Sophie talked about their angel, not the confusion and chaos along the city streets.

"She came down from heaven," Aaron said.

"What's her name?" Sophie asked.

Aaron thought a minute. "She wants to be unanimous."

Beth's lips twitched into a tiny smile. One day she would explain to Aaron the difference between "unanimous" and "anonymous," but not today.

That night after the children were tucked in bed, Beth sat beside her window and looked out into the city that had changed forever. Thousands had died that day. Thousands more were grieving for loved ones who would never come home. Yet God sent an angel to help a mother and two children who were not directly in harm's way. Beth knew her faith had grown enormously on the day that changed her country. Aaron was right: God is "unanimous"—he answers every prayer.

*W*hen disasters do not threaten us physically, we should still appeal to God to calm our fears and to comfort our families and us. God is greater than any evil that befalls humanity. In his mighty army, God always has angels to spare. The Bible tells us in Romans 8:31: "If God is for us, who can be against us?" (NIV). Through prayer, we learn the truth of his magnificent love for us. We may feel our need is small compared to the needs of others. But God expects us to turn to him in every situation with the faith of a child who believes, even when we cannot see the goodness and protection that surround us.

*P*ray without ceasing, let your love
  illumine the skies
That the darkness of man may drop away
And only the light of God show through.
Pray unto the Holy, with all your heart
  and soul
Pray for the shining light of guidance
That your path may be glorious with love.

ST. AUGUSTINE

When the righteous cry for help,
the Lord hears, and rescues them
from all their troubles. The Lord
is near to the brokenhearted, and
saves the crushed in spirit.

Psalm 34:17–18

With One Heart

Lord, today I join my prayer with prayers
of people all over the earth who long for
peace. We pray in many languages, but
with one sore heart at the plight of this
angry world. With so much war among
countries, communities, faith groups,
and even in families, it is sometimes
hard to hear your voice calling us to
reconciliation. Lord, help us put down
our weapons and learn to love one
another. Lord, help us live as brothers
and sisters in your holy peace.

You promise that where I am weak, you are strong, God. Help me stand on that promise today. When my faith falters, I depend on you to shore it up. When fear overwhelms me, I depend on you to say "fear not." When I procrastinate, tell me to "do it now." When I am angry, help me turn the other cheek. When I worry, I depend on you to remind me that worry is a waste of time and shows a lack of faith. I am not expecting an easy day. But with you beside me, difficult days can also be days of grace. Thank you for being with me. Amen.

*H*eavenly Father, I feel vulnerable today. Shadows cover my joy in being your beloved child. I know your light is brighter than all my cares, but I am not walking in your radiance. Please lead me away from this gray place and into the sunshine of your love. I need your help, God, to walk away from the shadows, and I need your strength for the journey.

For surely I know the plans I have for you, says the Lord, plans for your welfare and not for harm, to give you a future with hope. Then when you call upon me and come and pray to me, I will hear you.

Jeremiah 29:11–12

An Angel from Brooklyn

Kim traveled all the way from Brooklyn to
Nicaragua to answer a prayer. Actually, she
thought she was going to Nicaragua to direct a
video shoot for a charity that helped people in
the shantytowns of the poor Central American
country. It was her first video project, and she
wanted everything to go perfectly. Prior to her
trip, she worked with the charity's office in
Nicaragua to make sure they had chosen a good
family to feature. She called them four times
to work out the details, and she sent follow-up
e-mails to verify every part of the plan down to
the minute. After all, she was spending a large
chunk of the charity's budget to make the video,
and she did not want to waste a cent.

Kim arrived with the video crew on the
appointed day. A Nicaraguan government
staff person escorted the team through the
shantytown to the home of the family they had
selected for the film. They knocked on the door.
No one answered. They waited awhile, then they
knocked on a neighbor's door and asked where
the family might be. The neighbor shrugged.
They had packed up and moved out the night
before. No one knew where they had gone or

if they would return. Kim was distraught. She muttered a quick, ungracious prayer, "Lord, this is your money we are wasting. We need another family to film, and we need them now!"

Kim was unaware that in a one-room shanty nearby lived Blanca Rosa. She rose at 3:00 A.M. every morning to go to the market to buy ingredients for the pizzas she sold to support her three kids. It was her only source of income, and she was proud that with the little money she made she could feed her children every day. But she had to live day-to-day. She never made enough money to be able to save more than she needed for the next day's pizza ingredients and family meals.

That same morning, Blanca was robbed at knifepoint on the way to the market. The thief took 50 dollars, all the money she had in the world. She would not be able to buy ingredients today. She had no money to buy food for her children. How would she be able to run her business again?

Trembling and downhearted, Blanca returned home. After she recovered from her fright, she thought it over. Then she prayed. When she woke the children for school, she told them they were having a large serving of hope for breakfast. She added with conviction, "The Lord loves us and will provide our supper. You just watch and see what God does."

Meanwhile, the Nicaraguan staff person told Kim, "I know another family we may be able to tape, and they don't live far away. The mother's name is Blanca Rosa. I think you'll like her. Let's see if she is home."

Kim and the video crew followed her down the dirt paths between shanties. This was the poorest place Kim had ever seen. Blanca's shanty looked no better or worse than any others, and Kim quickly thanked God that Blanca was home.

Blanca did not tell them her sad story. She graciously agreed to talk on camera about her life, her children, her pizza business, and her faith in God. She and Kim quickly warmed to one another, and Kim was struck by the inner peace and joy this woman exuded despite her poverty. When the taping was done, Kim quietly pressed some money into her hand for being their star.

Blanca looked at the 50 dollars and said, "Good-bye, my angel from Brooklyn. You came on an airplane, but God bought your ticket." It was then that Blanca told Kim she had been robbed of exactly 50 dollars that morning.

Blanca and her friends still talk about the woman from Brooklyn, but they don't call her Kim; they call her "Blanca's Angel."

*H*ave you ever found yourself quite unexpectedly in the right place at the right time, although you had planned to arrive earlier or later—or to be somewhere else altogether? Instead of being frustrated at delays and last-minute changes of even the best-made plans, we should remember that God can change anyone's plans, particularly to answer a faith-filled prayer. You may be pleading with God to remove the obstacles to your plan, but he may have chosen you to help someone whose need is greater. And, yes, he will answer your prayers, too, perhaps in a way you cannot imagine. Amazing things happen when people pray. It can all come out right in the end.

One day…we shall gratefully see that God's greatest refusals were sometimes the truest answers to our prayers.

P. T. FORSYTHE, *SOUL OF PRAYER*

Never be lacking in zeal, but keep your spiritual fervor, serving the Lord. Be joyful in hope, patient in affliction, faithful in prayer. Share with the Lord's people who are in need. Practice hospitality.

Romans 12:11–13 NIV

A Precious Day

Dear God, this seems like another ordinary day—routine tasks, half-formed thoughts, hurried conversations, and many things left undone. Please help me see today as a precious day belonging to you and given to me for reasons I may never understand. The work you have for me today will go unnoticed by most and may seem unimportant to me. I ask you to send me into the world with an open heart and open hands and with an eagerness to serve you in every way I can.

Amen.

You made this day, Lord, so it will be good despite things that go wrong. No matter what today brings, I can rejoice and be glad because you are with me. Beneath any fears and pain, your steady hand will bring me through. My simple prayer is that tonight I will turn to you with a thankful heart and a shining nugget of gladness.

Thanks and Regrets

Heavenly Father, my day's work is done,
and I turn to you with gratitude and
regrets. I am thankful for each person I
encountered. I am grateful for food and
shelter and other basic things I take for
granted. I regret the times I failed you
by being less giving than you call your
people to be. I ask forgiveness for my
impatience and jaded thoughts. I pray for
peaceful, healing sleep and the grace to
be a better child of God tomorrow.

A "Grate" Mom

Erica's dedication to her career had nothing to do with the scarred tile floor of her poorly lit office. Its only window framed rusty iron burglar bars and a view of a crumbling brick wall. She had a mission, saving teens from gangs and drugs. Relentlessly, she banged on the elegantly carved doors of big corporations to encourage them into funding her program. She interrupted council meetings to make the city stretch its budget to include inner-city youth at grave risk of addiction, jail, and murder. At 35, she had made a life-changing difference in the lives of hundreds of once-hopeless, inner-city youth.

Kirk, her husband of 15 years, loved her dearly and gladly did more than his share of the household work. He was an avid supporter of her cause. He celebrated with her each time a child was rescued from a life of crime. He mourned with her when a child sank into the urban mire. But he wanted something for them both. On her 35th birthday, he decided it was time.

At an intimate dinner for two, in their little dining room, he watched Erica unwrap her gift. It was a beautiful, wooden picture frame with "Our Family" carved across the top. She frowned. "It's for three pictures," she said, "not two."

His desire for a child stunned her. It was not
in their plan. And, furthermore, how would she
find the time? She saw that the look on his face
was more than disappointment—it was grief.
After days of being polite with each other rather
than acting as the true partners they had been,
she began to realize that perhaps she was wrong.
She asked Kirk to pray with her so together they
could discern God's will.

But after a month, they admitted God was
not writing his will on the wall. They decided
the only thing to do was to step out in faith and
leave it up to God. Three weeks later, she wept
in utter confusion while the father-to-be rejoiced
over the results of her first pregnancy test. She
knew nothing about babies and too much about
teenagers and all the things that can go wrong.

Pregnancy was both a misery and a mystery.
Nausea, swollen feet, fatigue, and fear of being
a parent plagued her. The mystery was that she
was growing to love the child she had never
expected to have. The teens she counseled,
tutored, and bailed out of jail looked at her
differently now. Even the most sullen smiled
and congratulated her.

One day when she was eight months
pregnant, she walked into her office and found

a note: She was needed immediately in the café. She thought she read the note wrong, for when she walked into the café she saw it was decorated with streamers and balloons. Twenty teens—some homeless, some addicted, some considered hopeless by any measure but hers— had pooled their small change to give her a baby shower. And, happily, they had invited her husband.

One teen, whose juvenile criminal record was three inches thick, had baked the cake. Even though the boy was on parole, Erica had badgered a baker into giving him a job. Now, he had persuaded the baker to let him use the bakery's oven, ingredients, and pans to bake the cake. On the too-blue icing was bright pink script that read "To a Grate Mom." Erica was touched and said, "It's almost too beautiful to eat!"

Three of the teenage girls smiled proudly when she opened their gift, a little gown they had made in home economics and embroidered with bunnies. "You're all back in school?" said Erica. They had dropped out a year ago. Erica had not been able to convince them to do the hard work of graduating from high school.

"Been back three months," one of them said. "Wanted it to be a surprise for your party."

These teens, who didn't seem to know how to plan two minutes ahead, had been planning her party for three months? Erica buried her head in her husband's chest and sobbed.

"Happy tears," she was finally able to explain to her young friends. "I didn't know if I could be a good mom until you showed your faith in me."

After Erica gave birth to their baby girl, Kirk brought them home to a nursery filled with balloons. All were pink, except one that was a bright shade of blue. On it was written in hot pink: "To a Grate Mom."

*P*rayer is crucial when it comes to making major life decisions. Sometimes the answer is immediate and clear. Sometimes our prayers are met with silence. But within that silence is the invitation to take a leap of faith. Like a father teaching a child to be strong and confident, God lets go of our hand

and lets us take a step that we feel we are taking all alone. Do we trust him enough to take that step? When we make decisions with the faith of a child, God's hand is only a heartbeat away.

My Perfect Friend

You listen to my pleas when my heart is heavy, God, and you hear my praise when my heart is light. You accept me as I am every moment of every day. You stand beside me to help and heal, and you walk before me to guide me. You share my joy in each shining moment and lead me to your pastures of peace. Thank you, God, for being my perfect friend.

*P*ray always, while you eat and sleep.
   Pray in your dreams, that the
      prophets may appear
   And give you true vision.
   Pray that your road in life
   Will follow the footsteps of
      the Lord,
   That you may not mistake death for
      life nor sorrow for joy,
   That your soul, now a half-dead
      sparrow with broken wing,
   Shall be fed, and cured, until at the
      peak of health
   He begins his journey, the flight
      towards the sun.

                           AUTHOR UNKNOWN

*D*ear Lord, I remember a bedtime prayer of my childhood: "I pray the Lord my soul to keep." These simple words of a trusting child are all I need to say today. With my soul in your hands, nothing in this world can separate us. I often make it too complicated, Lord, with too many words. I make it so complicated that I confuse myself. Help me remember, Lord, that you answer my childhood prayer every day of my life. Amen.

Lovely Living

Father, help me remember to praise you
and thank you for the moments of my
days that lighten my spirit: the first glass
of fresh orange juice; the people
who greet me on the street; the
children flying down the sidewalk
on skateboards; a happy song on
the radio; the e-mail that makes me
smile; the friend who stops by for a chat.
If I counted the good moments and the
bad, the good would win—but who has
time for all that math? Yet, I need to take
time to thank you for the moments that
make lovely living of my ordinary life.

Spring Called

Kathy's divorce caught up with her one Sunday morning in early March. All winter she had followed her friends' advice to "keep on keeping on." She kept up with her job, children, house, and her Girl Scout troop. She learned how to do simple home repairs and how to maintain the car. She learned how to cook for four, not five, and how to live on a tight budget. But that morning her body felt like lead. Her mind was foggy, and her motivation was gone. If the house was to catch fire, she might drag herself out of bed. She felt guilty that her children were preparing their breakfast without her and was deeply touched that they sensed she needed to be alone. They deserved a special hug, but she could not move.

All morning Kathy lay in bed watching sunlight shift from wall to dresser to bookshelf. She felt a deep, scary emptiness where dreams once bloomed. After the children went out to play, the phone rang. It took every ounce of energy she had to walk to the kitchen and pick up the phone. "Yes!" she barked, not bothering to cover her annoyance.

Her friend Nancy said, "I was praying during church today and you popped into my head. Just calling to see how you're doing."

"Thanks for calling," Kathy said and hung up. She couldn't wait to get back under the covers. But she noticed the kids had run the dishwasher. The least she could do was put away the dishes. She moved slowly, reluctantly, but she was doing it for her children, so she finished the job. At last, she could go back to bed. But the children had sorted their dirty laundry in piles by the basement door. The least she could do was start a load of laundry.

When that task was finished, Kathy headed to bed, pausing to look out a window. The snow had melted, and a few buds were swelling. The ice in the birdbath had melted. The children were playing in light jackets, not coats, and their mittens lay stiffly on the radiator. The cold, bitter season had turned at last. Going back to bed would be returning to her cold, bitter season.

Kathy packed a picnic lunch and found her spring jacket. Her tennis shoes, behind a pile of boots, still had a few fall leaves on them. *When I wore them last, I was happy,* she thought, and she felt the emptiness again. Then a splotch of sunlight danced on her hand and distracted her.

To her children's delight, she told them to pile into the car. She drove to a nearby park. The wind was brisk, but the sun was warm. The food and fun were simple. Sandwiches and swings. Cookies and a slide. Lemonade and jokes. Lots of hugs and a sound Kathy had not made in months: laughter.

Their picnic was the opposite of the winter's hard work of slogging through her grief. Kathy was having fun. As they were cleaning up, she told her children that there would probably be some more sad times ahead but to remember they would have many good days like this. She saw in their eyes that they believed her, and she felt in her heart she was telling them the truth.

That night, after tucking the children in bed, Kathy called Nancy to thank her for her phone call. Kathy apologized for being so abrupt and told her friend that if she had not called Kathy would probably still be in bed.

"I wasn't going to call you," Nancy said. "I felt I was being nosy or intrusive. But a little voice in my head would not stop whispering 'call her, call her.'"

"That little voice was my wake-up call," Kathy smiled. "Happy springtime to you, my friend."

That still, small voice…how many times have we heard it and how many times have we ignored it? God doesn't send letters and e-mails from heaven. He expects his children to listen to the whispers of the spirit. We are called to love and serve one another. If a friend or loved one weighs heavily on your mind, don't just wonder how they are doing— make a phone call, write a letter, or visit them. You could be God's messenger. What a privilege to be chosen for such a heavenly task. Don't be too busy to do what the spirit is urging you to do.

*F*ather in Heaven, morning dawns in a peaceful sky, and the birds sound delighted to be alive. Help me take your peace down the road and into the workplace. Let me share your peace with all the hurting, yearning people I encounter today. The moments of peace you give me this morning will drift away like a whisper unless I put them into action and share them. Amen.

In the Garden

I come to the garden alone
    while the dew is still on the roses;
And the voice I hear, falling on my ear
    the Son of God discloses
And he walks with me, and he talks
    with me
And he tells me I am His own;
And the joy we share as we tarry
    there,
None other has ever known.

C. AUSTIN MILES

CHAPTER 7

Faith to Move Mountains

Lord, give me a faith in you like fire that is strong and unceasing. Fill me with the flame of your promise of eternal glory. Let me feel the warmth of your grace that brings me miracles and blessings. Let me bask in the glowing light of your merciful forgiveness that allows me the chance to try again when I have failed. Set me alight with a powerful faith, a faith in you, dear Lord, to move the mountains of my life. Amen.

The Gleam of Faith

The sun was shining on the hill
  Although on every side the rain
  Kept falling steadily and chill.
  But I looked upward and saw plain
  The whole hill glow as if on fire,
  Like revelation, like a dream
  That bids the dreamer come up
    higher.
  So sometimes through our gloom,
    a gleam
  Of faith comes flashing through
    the mind,
  And though it shortly fades away,
  It leaves a brighter world behind,
  Fairer by that remembered ray.

JAMES DILLET FREEMAN

*T*o believe in something enough that it cannot help but manifest is to know the power of faith. Just to imagine is not enough. You must back your imaginings with every ounce of courage, love, and conviction your heart can muster. That is when you will truly find faith.

> **Have faith in God. Truly I tell you, if you say to this mountain, "Be taken up and thrown into the sea," and if you do not doubt in your heart, but believe that what you say will come to pass, it will be done for you.**
>
> **Mark 11:22–23**

Empowered

Lord, my faith empowers me when I am feeling low and emboldens me when I am lacking in courage to face some unknown challenge. Thank you for faith! My faith encourages me when all looks hopeless and enlightens me when confusion and chaos are the order of the day. Thank you for faith! My faith enriches me when I feel empty and embraces me when I am so alone. Thank you for faith! Thank you, Lord, for your faith in me and for giving me the gift of faith in myself and in you. Amen.

*L*ord, may your kingdom come into my heart to sanctify me, nourish me, and purify me. How insignificant is the passing moment to the eye without faith! But how important each moment is to the eye enlightened by faith! How can we deem insignificant anything which has been caused by you? Every moment and every event is guided by you, and so contains your infinite greatness. So, Lord, I glorify you in everything that happens to me. In whatever manner you make me live and die, I am content. Everything is heaven to me, because all my moments manifest your love.

JEAN-PIERRE DE CAUSSADE,
"THE PASSING MOMENT"

Crossing That Bridge

Sherry felt the lump during a routine self-examination. She didn't want to panic, having felt small lumps in her breasts before that turned out to be cysts. Still, she couldn't help feeling frightened. This one was bigger and more defined.

It took her three weeks to make an appointment with her doctor, not because she was too busy but because she was too scared. Somehow she believed that if she kept putting it off the lump might disappear. It didn't. Her doctor felt the lump and ordered a biopsy for the following week. Sherry would have to wait and see if it was going to be simply another cyst. She felt as if she were sitting at an intersection waiting for the light to turn red or green, but it was stuck on yellow.

Sherry told her husband and her two best friends about the lump and the upcoming biopsy. She did not tell her mom or sister. She knew they would be worried and make her feel more panicky than she already was. Both women had fought breast cancer and won. Sherry now felt like a member of the club, but she preferred not to have to join. She would wait until the biopsy results came back before she told them.

The days leading to the biopsy opened up a whole slew of emotions Sherry had faced before with her mom and sister. But now she was the object of her own worry and fear. She had two daughters in grade school and could not bear to think about what might happen to her or to them. It was the one bridge she simply could not cross until she came to it.

The day of the biopsy, Sherry's friend, Lisa, drove her to the hospital. She waited there during the procedure and drove her home. Lisa stayed with Sherry the rest of the day until Sherry's husband came home. She helped make dinner for the couple and their two girls, who had not been told about Sherry's situation. There was no reason to worry them at this point.

In her mind, shadows danced to and fro, taunting Sherry with visions of what might go wrong, visions of cancer and disability and death. Sherry tried to keep her focus on what was directly in front of her, but the not-knowing and the waiting made her feel as if she were losing her mind.

A spiritual person, Sherry felt compelled to turn to God and pray for guidance. She did believe that God was loving and healing. The outcome of her biopsy was in God's hands now, and she had to have complete faith that the results would be what was meant to be. Perhaps there were lessons that she could learn only from having cancer. Perhaps this was all a test of her faith and trust.

Three days later, the phone rang. Sherry's stomach tightened; she knew it was her doctor. Her husband was home, and he looked at her with slight panic. She nodded, then walked over and picked up the receiver. She barely croaked out a hello, standing frozen as she listened to her doctor tell her the results.

Sherry quietly hung up the phone and turned to her husband. Tears were in her eyes, and he ran toward her. She stopped him and told him the lump was benign, and they embraced and held each other for a long, long time, weeping with relief and joy.

Later that night, Sherry sat on the couch and watched her husband and daughters playing. She smiled, knowing she could stop waiting and return to living again. She also knew something else: Her faith had made her strong, strong enough to face whatever test results she might have been given that day. She whispered a silent prayer of thanks to God and joined her family at play.

Where It Belongs

God, I am putting my faith in you in a way I have never done before. These troubles have taken their toll on me and my loved ones, and now I am ready, willing, and able to surrender my life to you. Do with me as you will, for I have faith that your will is for my best. Lead me where you desire, and I will be as an obedient child and follow, knowing that your guidance will never steer me down the wrong path. I am putting my complete trust and faith in you, God, where it belongs.

*I*t is easy to have faith when life is filled with happiness, comfort, and pleasure. When things are running smoothly, we know we are aligned with the spirit and walking the path we were meant to take. But as soon as things get difficult, we run for cover, begging for mercy and pleading with God for instant release from our challenges. How easily we forget that our faith keeps us strong through bad times just as in good times. It is like the promise two lovers make as they exchange marriage vows: to stay together in times of prosperity as well as lack, in times of sickness as well as health. Faith is our partner, and the promise is the same. We are never alone.

*M*y faith in you may waver, Lord, but
it never disappears. I may sometimes
wonder why you give me the challenges
you do, but I will not stop believing it
is for my highest good. I often wish
I could have things perfect all the time,
but I understand that you are molding me
to be better and stronger. Yes, sometimes
I get angry about the pain I am feeling,
but deep in my heart I know it is part of
the blessed miracle of life you have given
me, and I am grateful. Amen.

Today I Am!

Today I am alive; this gives me faith
for tomorrow.

Today I am healthy; this gives me
strength for when I am ill.

Today I am happy; this gives me
hope for what's to come.

Today I am whole; this gives me
power to move with ease in my
world.

Today I am brave; this gives me
courage to face any challenge that
may arise.

Today I *am!* And this gives me faith
to try to be the best I can be.

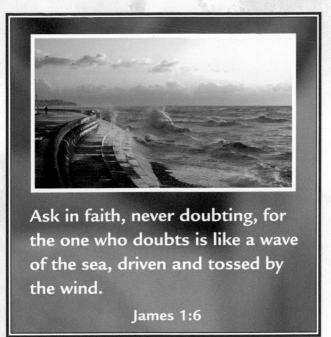

Ask in faith, never doubting, for the one who doubts is like a wave of the sea, driven and tossed by the wind.

James 1:6

You already have faith—each time you rise out of bed to face the challenges of the day. You already have courage—each time you go to bed at night ready to do it all over again tomorrow.

Taking a Stand

The moment Donna's mother and sister walked in, she felt anxious. They were there for a birthday party for Donna's two-year-old son, Mark, and she was not looking forward to the direction she knew the evening would take.

She loved her mother dearly, and she was close to her sister, Anne, but whenever the three of them got together, it inevitably turned into a forum where her mom and sister ganged up on Donna and criticized her for everything from her weight to her house cleaning to her recent divorce from an overbearing husband. Donna's dad had always defended her, but he had passed away a year ago. Now Donna had to defend herself alone.

This party would be no different. Within ten minutes, Donna's mother launched into a lecture about how dirty the sink was and how much easier life would be if Donna had stayed married. Then Anne chimed in, commenting on how much Mark was missing not having his father around. Usually, Donna would just grin and bear it. Never would she admit the true extent of the damage that her family's unkind criticisms had on her.

Two painfully long hours later, the birthday party was over, and Donna said good-bye to her mother and Anne. They hugged and kissed her, telling her they had a great time and would see her soon. Silently, Donna hoped it wasn't soon. She put a sleepy Mark to bed and sat up for hours on the couch, thinking about why she was the victim of their verbal abuse. She prayed for understanding, for enlightenment. If she could understand why they did it, she could deal with it better.

The following morning, Donna awoke with a start. She sat up in bed with a great clarity of mind. It suddenly became so perfectly clear, so in focus. She was the brunt of her family's hostility because she was changing her life for the better, and they were threatened by it! Anne's husband was a jerk, and Anne didn't have the courage to confront him or to leave him as Donna had done with her husband. Donna also realized that her attempts to lose weight and improve herself always met with her mother's resistance because her mother, who was also overweight, could never get over the fears that kept her from improving her own life.

With her new sense of clarity, Donna made a decision. It was a decision that would require all her inner fortitude, faith, and courage. She decided she would no longer be the victim and that her mother and sister would not be permitted to be a part of her life until they stopped their verbal abuse.

When her mother and sister did come by a week later, uninvited, Donna opened the door but did not let them in. They looked at her, startled, and Donna told them in no uncertain terms that they were not welcome in her home until they learned to respect her and her life choices.

She closed the door and sighed. She knew she would need to have faith in herself, in God, and in her loved ones that it would all turn out right in the end. No matter how long it took for her mother and sister to come around, Donna would stick to her guns and hold fast to her belief that she deserved to be treated with love.

It was many weeks before Donna received a phone call from either her mother or sister. They met for lunch and ended up having a deep, heartfelt talk that brought them closer together. Donna received their apologies, and they asked for her forgiveness. She hoped this was the beginning of a real relationship and that they truly would change. Ultimately, she would have to go on faith. Time would tell, but she was willing to wait and see.

*T*o "have faith" means so much more than just believing in something. To have faith means that we believe in something good, for ourselves and for the world around us, even when all our eyes can perceive is darkness and despair. Having faith means seeing peace where conflict currently exists. It means knowing love when hatred is the rule of the day. It means working for justice when all around us is evidence of the cruelty of unfairness. Faith is belief in what we cannot see, in what our hearts tell us joyfully is there.

*B*e not afraid of life. Believe that your life is worth living, and your belief will help create the fact.

WILLIAM JAMES, "THE PRINCIPLES OF PSYCHOLOGY"

*G*od, I have suffered much of late. Keep me from losing my way completely, for as long as I can see the light I can keep going. Restore hope to my heart, courage to my spirit, and strength to my body as I stand to face the trials in my life. Instill in me a deeper wisdom that knows I can, with your help, withstand the storm. Give me a greater faith that knows I can, with your love, grow from this experience and be better than I was before.

*F*aith is believing what you do not see; the reward of this faith is to see what you believe.

ST. AUGUSTINE

Silver Lining

Give me faith, Lord, to see the silver lining in any dark cloud. Show me how to discern your wisdom and your grace, even when all looks lost and I am feeling defeated by life's challenges. It is said that with you all things are possible and you will never give me more than I can handle. Help me to make my faith grow. Amen.

A Mustard Seed of Faith

They say if you have steadfast faith
The size of one mere mustard seed
That you can move a mountain high
And place it where you see the need.

They say having faith is the way
To manifest the dreams you dare,
But faith is far, far more than that—
It's knowing you're already there.

A New Beginning

Charlize called her husband, Josh, at his office and told him to come home as soon as possible. The cramping had come on slowly at first, and she did not want to alarm him, so she just said she was not feeling well and thought she should see the doctor.

It was her eighth month of a very difficult pregnancy. From the start, she had suffered from bleeding and cramping. She often thought she had miscarried, but always the pregnancy had continued. Her doctor smiled and told Charlize that her baby was quite a trooper, but it did little to relieve her fears each time a new problem arose.

Josh hurried home and rushed her to the hospital. She was bleeding heavily, and the cramping was so bad it made her double over. She felt everything inside her go numb as she was helped out of the car and wheeled into the ICU.

She was hemorrhaging, and the color drained from her skin as the surgical team moved her into the surgical arena. A nurse placed a mask over her face. Charlize fought as the anesthesia took effect, not wanting to give up control.

When Charlize opened her eyes, she was lying in a recovery room and Josh was sitting beside her. He had been crying, and she let out a weak moan, thinking the worst. But Josh told her that the baby, their little boy, had survived, just barely, and was now on his way to the Children's Hospital. Charlize wept, anguished that her baby was not there with them.

For four days, Charlize stayed in the hospital without being able to see her baby. Josh would go down to the Children's Hospital and come back with progress reports, which weren't good. The child, whom they named Ben, was premature and very weak. The doctors were giving him a 50/50 chance of survival. Charlize clung to that 50 percent chance.

She spent her hours praying quietly to God. She went through every emotion, from anger to ecstatic hope, and from despair to denial. When her husband was there, they held each other close, barely speaking about Ben, but both thinking only of him.

Charlize was allowed to go home on the fifth day. Josh drove her down to Children's Hospital to see Ben. They'd been told that their baby was having respiratory problems and he might not make it through the night. This visit possibly would be Charlize's only time to see the child she had wanted more than anything else on earth.

When Charlize saw her son for the first time, her heart burst with joy and broke with pain at the same time. He was so small and pale and weak. She bent down and whispered to him, knowing he couldn't hear or understand her. But she hoped that he could feel the love she was sending to him.

She wasn't sure what compelled her to say this to Ben, but Charlize felt the baby might be hanging on just to make her happy. So she lovingly told him that she wanted him to live more than anything, but if it was his desire to go to God, she would accept it. She closed her eyes and sang Ben a lullaby.

Visiting time ended, and Josh took his distraught wife home. Emotionally drained, they went to bed early. Charlize lay awake, praying again, except this time she asked God to give her the strength to handle the outcome, no matter what it would be. Her faith was strong, and she believed God could give Ben life, but only if it was God's will.

At daybreak, Josh was already awake and on the phone, asking the hospital nurse about Ben. He hung up and smiled at Charlize, then told her the good news. Ben was doing better; he was showing signs of improvement. They could visit

their new son that afternoon. Charlize closed her
eyes and whispered a prayer of thanks to God.

*F*aith is the strongest foundation upon
which to build a dream. It is the only
foundation that can withstand the forces
of nature and the fears of the intellect.
Faith stands up against all tests, all
challenges, all trials by fire. Faith is
backed by God, and there is no greater
power. With faith, we are able to endure
what we never thought we could. With
faith, we are surefooted as we make
our way through life. With faith comes
knowing that we are always grounded
in a solid and unmoving foundation of
truth, love, and divine guidance.

There will be times when we are asked to be more than we ever thought we could be, to do more than we ever thought we could do, and to give more than we ever thought we could give. Faith is knowing that we can and will rise to meet every challenge.

Lord, I look to you with total faith in your love and care for me. As an open-hearted spirit, I turn to you with complete faith in your strength and your dedication to my happiness and healing. With you watching over me, I feel safe in the knowledge that I am never alone and always deeply loved. Thank you.

Ready to Listen

What should I do, Father? I have placed
my will, my faith, and my hope in your
vision of perfection for my life. Thus,
I will trust whatever action you give me
to take. Your will for me is my desire, no
matter where in life it leads me. I have
faith that whatever comes my way, you
will help me to conquer it. I believe you
know what is best for me, and I am
ready to listen. Amen.

The Lord is faithful in all his words, and gracious in all his deeds. The Lord upholds all who are falling, and raises up all who are bowed down. The eyes of all look to you, and you give them their food in due season. You open your hand, satisfying the desire of every living thing. The Lord is just in all his ways, and kind in all his doings. The Lord is near to all who call on him, to all who call on him in truth. He fulfills the desire of all who fear him; he also hears their cry, and saves them.

Psalm 145:13–19

Be the Wind

Be the wind, O Lord, that blows away all
troubles from my path and clears the way
for me as I walk. Be the sun, O Lord, that
warms me when life's storms surround
me. Be the light, O Lord, that guides my
way when all around me the fog of doubt
hangs low and thick. Be the stars, O Lord,
that keep me looking upward in hope,
joy, and expectation of a better tomorrow.

Another Chance

Carol sat next to the phone, waiting for it to ring.
She had not heard from her teenage daughter,
Sara, in two days. In her heart, Carol knew Sara
had gone off with her boyfriend, Shane, on his
motorcycle. Despite Carol's warnings to keep
away from Shane, Sara had made up her mind
to, as she put it, "be herself."

Shane was one of those dangerous and irresponsible types, and Sara had become smitten with him. He was a high-school dropout that Sara had met at the mall where she worked. Carol had been against their dating, but Sara's father, who was in Europe on a long business trip, had caved in and told Sara she could go out with Shane.

Now Sara was probably on her way to Las Vegas to marry the bum, and Carol was at her wits' end. She had always been a great mother, loving and understanding, but she had also always known when to put her foot down. All Carol could do now was wait and have faith in her own mothering and in her daughter. Sara would come around or so Carol hoped with every fiber of her being.

Another day passed, and now Carol was beginning to panic. What if something had happened? Carol had tried to call Sara's cell phone several times, but Sara had not turned it on. She clearly did not want to be reached. Carol prayed to God that it was because her daughter was mad at her and not something sinister.

When the phone did ring, it was not the call Carol wanted. It was the police in the next state calling to inform her that her daughter had been in a terrible accident. She was in a hospital fighting for her life.

Carol felt her knees go weak. She could barely function and fumbled for the number of the hotel where her husband was staying. She dialed and, through her tears, left a message for him to come home immediately, that Sara had been in an accident.

A caring neighbor, Dee, volunteered to drive with Carol to the hospital. Three hours later, the attending surgeon told Carol that Sara had suffered internal injuries from the motorcycle accident. Luckily, she had survived. Unfortunately, Shane had not been wearing a helmet, having given his to Sara, and he had died as a result.

Carol broke down in sobs, and Dee led her over to a waiting room, where they sat holding each other. The entire time all Carol could do was pray to God. She asked him to help her daughter and the surgeons and to help her stay strong and have faith.

Carol's sister, Joan, arrived at the hospital. Dee had notified her, and she came and comforted her sister as they waited for word on Sara. Joan was a minister, and her presence immediately bolstered Carol's faith. Joan took out a book of inspirational poetry that she knew Carol liked and read to her sister about believing in God's love and healing and having faith that all will turn out for the best.

The poetry helped, especially when Carol was overcome with guilt for thinking badly of Shane. No matter how irresponsible he might have been, he was somebody's son, and Carol's heart ached for how his mother must feel. She vowed to keep believing that her daughter would make it through to live and love again.

The surgery took seven long hours, but when the surgeon came into the waiting room, he was smiling. He told Carol that Sara would recover, but it would take some time. Her daughter would have to remain in the hospital for a few days before she could go home. Carol thanked him profusely for saving Sara and asked to see her.

Sara was heavily sedated, but her eyes flickered at the sight of her dear mother. Carol sat beside her for the rest of the day, quietly thanking God over and over for giving her another chance to be Sara's mom.

Faithful One

God, I am your faithful one, who will
never surrender, never give in. For I know
you are always with me and I will never
have to handle any tragedy alone. You
are my source of all good, all strength, all
hope, all love, and I turn to you now for
the power that makes all things new again.
I am your faithful one, God, and I live to
fulfill your will, no matter where it leads
me or what I may have to face. I shall
walk without fear, move without doubt,
and live without confusion, for you are
my light, and I am your faithful one.

So we are always confident; even though we know that while we are at home in the body we are away from the Lord—for we walk by faith, not by sight.

2 Corinthians 5:6–7

*H*ave mercy on me, Lord, for I am frightened and filled with doubt. I know you said I could always put my faith and trust in you, but it is hard when I cannot see you, or touch you, or hear your voice clearly. Help me to discern your subtle guidance and to embrace your presence in everything around me. Show me that you are always in the midst of my life. Thank you, Lord.

Just as a carpenter uses tools to create a beautiful piece of furniture, we can use faith as the tool that allows us to build the life we dream of. With trust in our Lord, we realize that all our actions are guided by someone who knows what is best for us. Confused thinking turns into right action as we move with a newfound confidence toward our goals. Faith is a reliable tool we can carry with us at all times, and it requires no expertise or how-to manual. All faith requires is that we keep our minds and hearts open to receive the wisdom and the blessings of our Lord, for he wants our highest good.

Yet, in the maddening maze of things,
And tossed by storm and flood,
To one fixed trust my spirit clings;
I know that God is good!…
I know not where His islands lift
Their fronded palms in air;
I only know I cannot drift
Beyond His love and care.

JOHN GREENLEAF WHITTIER,
"THE ETERNAL GOODNESS"

These trials are only to test your faith, to see whether or not it is strong and pure. It is being tested as fire tests gold and purifies it—and your faith is far more precious to God than mere gold.

1 Peter 1:7 LB

CHAPTER 8

Someone to Lean On

You have shared your strength with me, God. Through your testing, you have shown me how to withstand some of the painful experiences of life. Enable me to share this knowledge, offering honest counsel and reasons for hope to others. Do not let me pass by someone in need of your strength because I am too busy. You have never been too busy to help me.

If the Lord had not been my help, my soul would soon have lived in the land of silence. When I thought, "My foot is slipping," your steadfast love, O Lord, held me up. When the cares of my heart are many, your consolations cheer my soul.

Psalm 94:17–19

Hearing with the Heart

Throughout all the trials in my life,
Father, you have always sent me people
with ears to hear the outcry of my
soul. Sometimes they have listened
without comment and just let me
vent my frustration. Other times they
have been helpful with their words of
encouragement and hope. Let me be one
of those people, who can listen with the
ears and the heart. Bless me with the gift
of listening so that I might, in turn, pass
on the blessings of consolation to others.

*L*ord, you challenge us to feed the
hungry, care for the sick, clothe the
naked, welcome the stranger, and visit
those in prison. We are also to encourage

the fainthearted and help the weak.
That's a tall order, Lord. Can I, personally,
do all that? Maybe not; but on the other
hand, maybe there are ways. Give me
your light and your strength, Lord, and
I'll do my best. Amen.

A Heart for Kids

From his front porch, 25-year-old Bart gazed
at the snow-covered mountains, lost in thought.
Winter was bleak in his small Vermont town.
Hilly roads were difficult for cars to navigate
without chains, so there was little traffic this
Saturday morning.

Young boys loitered around downtown with
nothing to do. The town had no movie theater,
bowling alley, roller rink, or game arcade. The
hottest ticket was the high school basketball
game. They found plenty to do in the spring and
summer, even fall, when local farmers hired them
for picking produce or maple sugaring. But in
winter there was nothing but firewood boxes to
fill or chickens to feed.

Only a few families had enough money to afford equipment for winter sports, so mostly the boys just hung out. Sometimes they went sliding on beat-up, hand-me-down sleds or makeshift barrel-stave skis. But they were growing too big for that. They needed some kind of organized activities to keep them out of mischief, Bart concluded.

Bart, a clerk in his family's furniture store, hoisted his skis on his shoulder and hiked up the road a mile to the town's old rope ski tow. From the top of the 300-foot hill, he began his descent. He loved the exhilarating sensation of flight that skiing gave him and wished all kids could experience it.

A caring young man, Bart was always on the lookout for ways God could use him. When he returned home from the slopes that afternoon, an idea began to form in his mind. Bart called his skiing friend Mike, who taught at the local high school, and bounced the idea off him. That night, they made plans for the area's first Boys Club, dedicated to winter sports, hiking, and woodlore.

The following week, Bart made the rounds of the town's businesses, soliciting funds for his Boys Club. He also collected from organizations and individuals, anyone willing to contribute to his cause. Then he invited the boys, ages 10 and up, to their first meeting. He laid out his plans for activities that included both indoor and outdoor sports.

Each Saturday, Bart spent the day with these boys, taking them on hikes in the woods, sledding, involving them in gymnastics and basketball. In a short time, Bart had collected enough money to buy inexpensive skis for all the boys in the group, and skiing was added to the program.

Sometimes they'd go to the local hill, and other times Bart would borrow a station wagon and take them to another town with higher slopes for additional instruction and fun.

Years later, as adults, the Boys Club members regarded Bart's role in their lives with heartfelt gratitude. One of the boys, Norm, went on to become a world-class skier. Now a consultant for a ski equipment company, Norm knew that without Bart there was no way the boys could ever have afforded skis; nearly everyone in town had been too poor. Norm owed his career to him.

Howard, also a Boys Club member, continued to live in the small Vermont town. He said that an entire generation of boys had looked to Bart for leadership and friendship. Bart gave them his time and attention. He listened to them and taught them things like responsibility and loyalty to God and country. He was like their big brother.

Bart also impressed upon the town fathers the importance of being involved with their sons' activities. Fred, another of the boys, remembered the time his dad helped him make ski poles from broomsticks, with pieces of metal on the bottom and leather loops on the handles. It was the first time his dad had paid so much attention to him. The other boys were so envious that they went home and convinced their dads to do the same.

On a recent trip to his hometown, Fred made it a point to visit Bart and let him know how grateful he was for Bart's work with the boys. Bart just grinned and nodded his head. "Yeah, I've heard that a few times," he said, then changed the subject.

> **The Lord is my rock, my fortress, and my deliverer, my God, my rock in whom I take refuge, my shield and the horn of my salvation, my stronghold.**
>
> **Psalm 18:2**

Although modest about it, Bart had expanded their world. He was a rock-solid, reliable guy with a heart for kids. He was their role model and someone they could count on. They would never forget him.

Pour Out Love

Father, you have blessed me with
skills and gifts to enrich my life.
Please show me the ones I can use in
service to you. As I encounter those who
need to be supported and upheld,
may I offer my ears to listen, my arms
to hug, and my shoulders to cry on.
Let me praise you with my offerings
throughout all my days. O Lord of great
compassion, stir in me the love that only
you can give and help me pour it out on
those who need it most.

Out in the wilderness, the Israelites had to be reminded there would never cease to be people in need on the earth and that they must open their hands to the poor and needy neighbors in their land (Deuteronomy 15:11). In our self-centered society, the same reminder can apply to us today. Often the needy include not just the poor but the poor in spirit. Sometimes the two go hand in hand. God wants us to open our hearts to anyone in need, be the need physical, emotional, or spiritual. When we do so, we are following his command to "Love your neighbor as yourself" (Leviticus 19:18).

You discover your own worth when you give yourself away in the service of those who need you.

All praise to Him who now hath turned
  My fears to joys, my sighs to song,
  My tears to smiles, my sad to glad.
  Amen.

ANNE BRADSTREET

My neighbors have so little, God. I want to help them, but they are proud of their independence. Please show me what I can do to help without making them feel like a charity case. I ask you to make me sensitive to the small deeds I can perform without making them feel I am robbing them of their dignity. Help me to bring joy and hope to their lives. Amen.

Count on Carrie

"What time do you report to the hospital?" Kim asked Aunt Elsa, as she made plans to accompany her and be present during her surgery.

"My pre-op workup is at 5:00 A.M.," she answered. Kim hesitated, calculating what time she'd have to be up to get ready and make the two-hour drive to Elsa's town.

Aunt Elsa chuckled, "Early, huh? For you that would mean getting up at 2:30 A.M."

Kim started to assure her she didn't mind, but she was interrupted.

"It's okay. You don't have to come that early. The surgery isn't until 11:00 A.M. My friend Carrie lives right here in town, and she's offered to take me. You can meet us at 10:00."

It wasn't the first time Carrie, a widow, had escorted someone to the hospital. She had been doing it for three years, mostly for people in her church who were alone or had no one nearby they could lean on. Carrie had been a hospital employee, but a chronic illness had forced her to retire prematurely.

After a few months at home, Carrie had become restless. She did some volunteer work at church but wanted to do more. She began thinking about what skills she had that she could use to help others. There weren't many.

Then Carrie's pastor told her about a church member who was scheduled for a hospital procedure. The man was elderly and very nervous about finding his way around the huge hospital complex.

"I can take him," Carried offered.

With her expertise, she was able to help the gentleman successfully negotiate his way through the building. The man was so grateful that he cried.

Carrie got a glimmer of an idea—she could do this for other people as well. She knew her way around the hospital, which was a big help because the complex had been renovated so often. There were lots of extra nooks and corners. She knew all the hard places to find and which elevators to take where. She also knew the scheduling procedures, the personnel, and where to go for information.

Carrie began to check in with her pastor once a week to find out who was slated for surgery or a hospital visit and might need help. Sometimes there were two or three in one week. With their permission, she contacted the people who lived

> **The Lord is good to all, and his compassion is over all that he has made.**
>
> **Psalm 145:9**

alone or had no one in the immediate area and asked if she could help them. Most of the time, they replied with a resounding "yes!"

Not only did Carrie help patients through admission, pre-op, and recovery, she also went back to visit them several times a week. She used her downtime to go home and feed the dog, take her medications, and talk to her daughter and grandchildren on the phone. Sometimes she took a quick nap.

Another advantage for Carrie was knowing many of the doctors from whom she could obtain procedural information about the patients. Her awareness of these facts helped the patients feel more relaxed.

Sometimes after surgery, the patients learned they needed to go to rehab appointments or schedule chemotherapy treatments. Carrie whipped out her pocket calendar and penciled in the dates. Then she either showed the person where to go or drove them there. If she couldn't stay during the entire session, she dropped off the patient and returned later to pick them up.

"I don't know what I'd do without Carrie's help," said Aunt Elsa, who was diagnosed with cancer after her surgery. "My chemo schedule is irregular, and I have to get a blood test every week the day before my treatment. Sometimes my chemo is cancelled because of test results. Carrie helps me keep it all straight; otherwise, I'd be hopelessly confused."

As Aunt Elsa's closest living relative, Kim was grateful to Carrie, too. Kim could look after her own family, including her elderly mother, and step in only during emergencies.

For Carrie, helping patients through the hospital maze had become a way of life. It wasn't like having a regular job or even a regularly scheduled volunteer job. She had lots of freedom. There was plenty of time for her own appointments. If she had something else she must do, she tried to work around all their schedules.

Despite Carrie's serious medical condition, she considered spending so much time and effort in this way to be good therapy. When she was helping others, she didn't have time to think of herself and her problems.

Grateful patients or relatives who try to thank Carrie or make a fuss over her get a hug and the response, "It's just something I think God wants me to do."

*A*re you a person to whom others come for help and support in times of trouble? Do you make yourself available—approachable? The apostle Peter encourages Christians to use the gifts God has given them to serve one another (1 Peter 4:10–11). Further, we are to use whatever resources the Lord provides, not only to help others but also to glorify him.

God made us in his image. As his children, we are all part of the human family. Who would not make an effort to rescue a family member in need?

> **Blessed be the God and Father of our Lord Jesus Christ, the Father of mercies and the God of all consolation, who consoles us in all our affliction, so that we may be able to console those who are in any affliction.**
>
> **2 Corinthians 1:3–4**

Look around you. Is there a situation in which you can use one of your gifts? Can you speak out for someone more timid than yourself? Do you have a listening ear or the gift of encouragement? Use your gifts to help others. God promises to give you his strength.

God blesses those who give calmness to the distraught, strength to the weak at heart, and comfort and solace to the ailing.

Prayer for God's Help

O God, from whom to be turned is
    to fall,
to whom to be turned is to rise,
and with whom to stand is to abide
    for ever;
grant us in all our duties your help,
in all our perplexities your guidance,
in all our dangers your protection,
and in all our sorrows your peace,
through Jesus Christ our Lord, Amen.

St. Augustine

An elderly relative is alone and in need of an advocate, Lord, as she enters the hospital for surgery. She lives far away and has no one else. Yet my family will be neglected if I decide to help her.
I remember what a positive presence she was in my life when I was a child. How do I balance the needs of my family with the needs of this precious person? Help me find a way to be her support, Lord. Let me be your presence in her life. Help me balance my obligations to make room for one more.

*F*ather, you have called us to be our brothers' and sisters' keeper. I have lived with those words since I was a small child. You have given me so much, Lord. How can I ignore your gifts and ignore the whispers of my heart? I cannot. Help me, Lord, to be obedient to your call. Amen.

Don't Judge a Book by Its Cover

Zack always thought of his uncle Norm as a stern, gruff person. He had been like that since he returned from World War II. The army had drafted Norm a month before he reached the cutoff age of 32. Now he seemed like an old man at 36.

Norm worried about everything: the government, prices of goods, his health, and his boss. He was always looking over his shoulder, expecting to be fired any day so a younger person with a lower salary could take his place. Of course, it never happened.

It seemed strange to Zack that such a person could be considered someone to depend on and lean on, but it turned out to be true. Norm would forever be his hero because of what he did the summer Zack was 14.

Uncle Norm was a bachelor, the only member of his family to remain single. Thus, he became the self-appointed caretaker of his widowed mother, Zack's grandmother. She did the cooking and cleaning; Norm did the chores and earned the living for both of them. He put up with her nagging, and she tiptoed around him when he was in a quiet mood. It was a workable arrangement.

Soon he gathered up his meager savings and decided to finish building the modest two-bedroom house that he had begun before entering the service. It was located just outside the city limits, and the entire family pitched in to help on weekends. By spring the house was in livable condition.

Grandma and Norm moved in, planted a huge garden, and considered themselves lucky to be owners of a little house in the country. They existed contentedly, with Norm finishing the inside of his home and Zack's gregarious grandma making friends with the neighbors. They joined a church in their new neighborhood, and Uncle Norm even made time for his hobbies of woodcarving and stamp collecting.

A few months later, the unexpected happened. Grandma's two older sisters, both maiden ladies, learned they were to be evicted from their tiny attic flat in the city. The new owners intended to fix up the apartment for their newly married son. With the sisters' measly pensions, they had nowhere to go.

The family scrambled to help search for an apartment and a solution to the problem. While

Zack's aunt was struggling with her new role as mother, his mom and dad had their hands and house full with their family of five. Again, the solution rested on Uncle Norm's shoulders.

Norm brooded but not for long. He looked at the problem from all angles and made his decision: He could not abandon these ladies. He would build an addition to his newly finished house and take in his two elderly aunts.

> **I lift up my eyes to the hills—from where will my help come? My help comes from the Lord, who made heaven and earth.**
>
> **Psalm 121:1–2**

The women cried for joy. Zack's uncle pulled his recently stored tools from the crawl space beneath the house and started all over again. He began a race to finish adding a room before his aunts' lease was up.

Zack was old enough to understand the sacrifice Uncle Norm was making. As a child, Norm had suffered through polio. He wore thick glasses and had a weak, underdeveloped arm. Yet he was drafted at age 32 and spent four years in the army—much of it overseas—with comrades nearly half his age. After his discharge, he had looked forward to a quiet, private existence.

Norm was to enjoy neither quiet nor privacy. He and Zack's dad finished the house addition, and his aunts were welcomed to their new home. He stretched his modest income to support four people instead of two.

Zack had thought Uncle Norm was gruff, but he was wrong. Norm was simply a very serious and responsible human being. Beneath his gruff exterior was a caring man on whom three older ladies could lean for the rest of their days.

We all need someone to lean on. In several places in the Old Testament, we are told the Israelites leaned on the Lord, and in fact, the Psalmist says, "Upon you I have leaned from my birth" (Psalm 71:6). In many ways, God has invited us to call upon him and lean on him in times of trouble or sorrow. He has promised to help and comfort, to rescue and revive us, and to do great things for us. God wants us to come to him—to let his strength be our strength and his hope be our hope.

You have commanded us to honor our parents, Lord, and I have tried to do that. They have willingly, happily taken care of me throughout my childhood and beyond. Now the situation is reversed, and they require my care. It is difficult tending to the needs of children and parents at the same time, yet you give me strength. Even as their care becomes more complicated and their needs increase, help me to be true to my promise to love and honor them all their days. Amen.

For the Beauty of the Earth

For the beauty of the earth,
For the glory of the skies;
For the love which from our birth,
Over and around us lies;
Lord of all, to Thee we raise
This, our hymn of grateful praise.

For the joy of human love,
Brother, sister, parent, child;
Friends on Earth and friends above,
For all gentle thoughts and mild;
Lord of all, to Thee we raise
This, our hymn of grateful praise.

FOLLIOTT S. PIERPONT

Someone God Can Count On

Jan had never heard of Habitat for Humanity when her husband, Scott, signed them up for a week of building and rehabbing houses in northern Michigan.

The area was rich with magnificent scenery—cool green pine and cedar forests, blue lakes, and huge golden sand dunes. However, it was located in the poorest county in the state, and few residents could spare the time to stand around and admire nature's beauty. They were too busy trying to make a living.

Habitat for Humanity International was founded in 1976 by Millard Fuller. He devised a model for building houses for the poor at low cost and with interest-free mortgages. To achieve this, he invited volunteers to do the work and to dig into their pockets for contributions to buy the materials and equipment. He also required the prospective owners to put 500 hours of their own "sweat equity" into working on the house themselves. Fuller's model has worked ever since.

Jan and Scott volunteered through their church and arrived on-site along with 30 others. To save money, they camped nearby, sleeping in their van and making meals over a campfire.

The money they saved went for the purchase of lumber, nails, paint, and an electric saw they used during the week. The gifts donated by the number of people present added up to a significant contribution.

On the first day, each person was assigned to work on one of the houses. Jan was very apprehensive about her ability to help, but by the end of the week, she and the other novices became pros as the houses were built. It was a miracle!

> **The Lord is my strength and my shield; in him my heart trusts; so I am helped, and my heart exults, and with my song I give thanks to him.**
>
> **Psalm 28:7**

Scott found that meeting the families who needed the boost was a real motivator. They seemed like ordinary folks who were down on their luck. One couple with two children had become impoverished because of the wife's chronic illness. She was uninsurable, and the medical bills took most of the husband's earnings.

The second house Jan and Scott worked on was for a single mother who had escaped an abusive spouse. She and her two boys came often during the week to watch the foundation being poured and the framework going up. They dug

in with enthusiasm and helped everywhere they
could.

The couple felt as though they were working
"as unto the Lord" as they hammered, sawed,
sanded, painted, and strung electrical wire. The
thought of that family moving into a house of
their own with an interest-free mortgage made
them work all the harder. Their work had a face
to it. They worked hard all day, then had time for
dinner, a worship service, and socializing later.
They found the experience wonderful, working
together with people from all walks of life to help
strangers build houses.

Jan and Scott were especially touched by
the plight of a grandmother who was trying
to care for her two small grandchildren in a
rusty, broken-down house trailer. Her daughter,
the children's mother, had been murdered by
her husband who was now in jail. The woman
helped by serving them cups of water. The
children eagerly helped by fetching tools and
other building material for their new house and
by carting away trash.

The Habitat projects were achieved by
a network of people helping people: The
homeowners could lean on the workers and the

workers could lean on each other and on God. The volunteers all understood that as they were building houses they were also helping to build up families.

Jan and Scott discovered it to be a valuable lesson: to know that someone was depending on them to help make their dreams come true and that each of them was a person who is dependable—someone God can count on.

Send Me

I need your help, Lord, to make a decision. Do I take a vacation in some exotic land, far from the stresses of my daily life, or do I trade my leisure for the opportunity to build a home for a needy person? You have showered your blessings upon me and have always provided me with hope. Can I do less for my impoverished neighbors? You have said that the poor will always be with us and we are to offer them a hand. Even if it means discomfort and inconvenience, Lord? Help me to take your people into my heart. Make me willing to answer, "Here I am, Lord; send me."

*G*od is good, showing compassion over all that he has made. "All" includes the lovely and the unlovely, the rich and the poor, the good and the bad. If, as Paul says, we are to be "imitators of God" (Ephesians 5:1), we must be ready to show compassion and love to all of God's children. As Mother Teresa liked to point out, when we minister to the impoverished, the wretched, and the unlovable, we are ministering to Christ in disguise.

You are the light of the world. . . .
Let your light shine before others,
so that they may see your good
works and give glory to your
Father in heaven.

Matthew 5:14, 16

*M*oses, a modest shepherd, became the reluctant leader of the Israelites and rescued them from slavery. Ruth, suddenly a widow in a foreign land, assumed the complete care of her distraught mother-in-law. The Good Samaritan, scorned by the Jews, took responsibility for a wounded neighbor when everyone else had passed him by. These were three entirely different situations, yet in each we see a person letting himself or herself be used by God to bring physical, emotional, and spiritual support to their fellow humans. Friend, relative, or stranger, each of them was a person of compassion, ready to serve others. It doesn't matter who we are or where we live; God can use us all to comfort his people.

Show Me What to Do

You are the rock to which we cling,
Father. Let me be an example of your
presence in the world to let others know
you are there. Show me what I can do to
bring your healing touch to the weak and
downtrodden so they can smile again.
Amen.

*W*hy did God give me hands, if not to reach out and touch someone who is hurting?

Why did God give me speech, if not to offer words of comfort to someone who is sad?

Why did God give me a heart, if not to share it with someone whose heart is breaking?

Do not fear, for I am with you, do not be afraid, for I am your God; I will strengthen you, I will help you, I will uphold you with my victorious right hand.

Isaiah 41:10

CHAPTER 9

Forgiving Is Living

*I*t awes me, Lord, that your love is so large that it forgives the greatest sins so completely that they are erased. I cannot erase the memory of my sins or the memory of those who sinned against me. It is only through you that I can forgive others and myself. Please take the sting out of my memories by teaching me to draw so close to you that I will remember every day how much you love me.

*W*here there is charity and wisdom, there is neither fear nor ignorance. Where there is patience and humility, there is neither anger nor vexation. Where there is poverty and joy, there is neither greed nor avarice. Where there is peace and meditation, there is neither anxiety nor doubt.

ST. FRANCIS OF ASSISI

*T*hose who forgive most shall be most forgiven.

WILLIAM BLAKE

Then Peter came to Jesus and asked, "Lord, how many times shall I forgive my brother or sister who sins against me? Up to seven times?" Jesus answered, "I tell you, not seven times, but seventy-seven times."

Matthew 18:21–22 NIV

Forgive

If I have wounded any soul today,
If I have caused one foot to go astray,
If I have walked in my own willful way,
Dear Lord, forgive!

If I have uttered idle words or vain,
If I have turned aside from want or
    pain,
Lest I myself shall suffer through the
    strain,
Dear Lord, forgive!

Forgive the sins I have confessed to
    Thee;
Forgive the secret sins I do not see;
O guide me, love me and my keeper be,
Dear Lord, Amen.

C. MAUDE BATTERSBY

Leading Ladies

Audrey drove a second time around the block where Deanna lived. She felt excited, fearful, and ashamed. Beside her were three very belated gifts: a wedding present, a size four ballerina costume with a "Welcome, Baby Girl" card, and a size six superhero costume with a "Congratulations on Your Baby Boy" card. She and Deanna had been best friends in high school where they were known as the "drama queens." They had shared a passion for acting and dreams of a star-studded future. They landed leading roles in every school play and practiced acting in their spare time. The week after graduation, they had planned to head for New York City and fame.

At their graduation party, Audrey felt like a seaworthy yacht, ready to be launched along with her sister ship. As the party wound down, though, Deanna grew quieter. Finally, she confessed that Mike had proposed and her next role would not be as a leading lady but as a wife and mother. In a cold fury, Audrey swore she would never speak to her again.

In New York, living their dream alone, Audrey's excitement was laced with fear. The dream unraveled slowly as she joined the ranks of unemployed actresses waiting on tables and doing routine temporary jobs. Some weeks she had to live on ramen noodles in order to pay the rent on the one-room hovel she shared now and then with temporary boyfriends. She tore up Deanna's wedding invitation and later her birth announcements. When Audrey's phone was not disconnected, she hung up on Deanna when she called.

Now Audrey drove around the block one more time before facing the dirge she had made of their once lyrical friendship. She had stopped blaming Deanna for her failures a few years ago. She had faced the fact she would never be a star and asked her parents to send her to college. Audrey became a high school drama teacher and was surprisingly happy with her job. She still missed Deanna but felt she had behaved too hatefully for Deanna to ever love her again.

She threw the invitation to their high school's tenth reunion in the trash. Teaching at school the next day, she overheard two young women in her class planning their future as movie stars. Audrey's heart ached. She decided to go to the high school reunion but knew she would have to see Deanna before the event.

Juggling the three wrapped gifts, Audrey rang her friend's doorbell. Deanna's look of astonishment turned to joy as she hugged Audrey, packages falling to the floor. "Can you, please…can you…forgive me?" Audrey stammered, tears streaming down her face. Deanna's reply was a stronger hug. She wiped Audrey's tears with the tail of her maternity top.

Soon the ballerina and the superhero were running around the house acting their little hearts out while the two women shared their struggles and triumphs of the past decade. Deanna insisted that Audrey cancel her hotel reservation and spend the night. Her husband Mike, a naval officer, was on a three-month tour of duty somewhere in the Pacific.

> **Do not judge, and you will not be judged; do not condemn, and you will not be condemned. Forgive, and you will be forgiven; give, and it will be given to you.**
> Luke 6:37–38

The next morning, Deanna said she was not going to the reunion that night. "Eight months pregnant and without a date," she sighed. "What fun would that be? I won't be a rotund third wheel on your romantic evening."

"Huh?" Audrey said. "I haven't had a date in six months. I assumed we'd go together."

"I honestly don't have anything to wear, and I can't afford a party dress," confessed her friend.

Audrey thought for a moment, then held up her index finger.

"Oh, no!" Deanna said, recognizing their old sign. "You have a plan."

"Remember what Scarlet O'Hara did with the velvet drapes?" asked Audrey, recalling the yard sale signs she'd seen in the neighborhood.

That night the "drama queens" attended their ten-year reunion. Deanna wore an elegant satin dress made from yard-sale curtains they'd hastily transformed. Before a full house of former classmates, Audrey and Deanna played their finest roles ever: best friends since freshman year. They wowed the crowd.

God forgives our every sin if we just ask him—his love is that enormous and complete. We can ignore him for decades or turn from him in hate, and still he forgives us the moment we ask. This is a truth we are taught, and it is a truth every soul knows no matter how deep we may bury it. But when it comes to friends, we are not assured that forgiveness will be offered. It is scary to initiate a reunion and say, "I am sorry." A door may be slammed in your face. Yet human love is often stronger and deeper than we can imagine. We must take the risks or suffer forever from wondering what joys we are missing because we were afraid to take a chance.

Mending a Friendship

I hurt someone today, God. I can't find
the words to tell them how deeply
I regret my thoughtless, unkind act.
Saying "I'm sorry" doesn't seem like
enough, because I'm more than sorry—
I'm ashamed. It seems that nothing will
make this right. I feel that something
precious we had between us is gone
forever. With your guidance and love,
I know forgiveness is possible. But I'm
the one who needs to be forgiven. I need
your strength to help me mend this
relationship. Please show me how,
Lord, for all I can see right now is a
big void where I once had a
friendship that gave me joy.

*H*oly God, thank you for the people in my life who love me in spite of my failings, who forgive me when I am thoughtless, and who never hold a grudge. Being with them is a little taste of heaven. You know me even better than they do; you know every secret and every thought. Yet you love me unconditionally. Thank you for giving me family and friends who reflect your love along my earthly path. Help me to grow in love and forgiveness that I may reflect this love to others more purely and often. Amen.

*W*e cannot create a new beginning
But we can work toward a new ending.

AUTHOR UNKNOWN

*A*n apology
Is a friendship preserver,
Is often a debt of honor,
Is never a sign of weakness,
Is an antidote for hatred,
Costs nothing but one's pride,
Always saves more than it costs,
Is a device needed in every home.

AUTHOR UNKNOWN

A Saturday Mother

Sadie hugged one-year-old Adam in her arms and kissed his freshly washed face. "Time to get your coat on," she said reluctantly, "and kiss Daddy good-bye."

The child wiggled off her lap and ran to his father, who gave him a big hug.

"See you next week, buddy," said Tom.

He sounded wistful. Adam was their Saturday child, their only child, and his mother, Alice, had just pulled her car into the driveway.

Sadie had been married to Tom for more than two years. She thought it was getting easier to face Alice, his ex-wife. Alice was a good mother, she had to give her that. Almost two years ago, Tom and his ex had indulged in a one-night stand. Sadie's rage had been as strong as her grief at her husband's betrayal. Alice's pregnancy had been the final blow. To forgive her husband would have meant she had to forget his infidelity. But how could she forget when his child was growing in Alice's womb? She felt that trying to work toward a reconciliation was doomed.

Yet Sadie persevered. She believed her husband loved her as much as he said he did. She knew she would never be able to respect him if he did not meet his obligation to his child. That obligation required being a father: spending time with the child and paying part of his support. She had little hope their marriage could be saved. She was too wounded, and her heart had hardened.

But when Alice put the week-old infant in her arms, Sadie's heart softened, and she burst into tears. This living proof of the grave sin against her was an innocent babe. As a woman, how could she hate this child? She could either love Adam or leave her husband so she would never have to see the child again. She chose to do the hard work of staying and loving.

Saturdays were difficult at first. She and Tom knew nothing about babies, but Alice was a patient teacher. She stayed long enough to teach them how to change Adam's diapers, feed him, burp him, and comfort him when he cried. Every Saturday she told them the new things he had learned and coached them in practical parenting matters.

"Better take off those dangling earrings," Alice had cautioned, pointing to Sadie's small pearl earrings. "He'll yank your earlobe off right along with them." And when he started crawling, she asked, "You've moved all the cleaning supplies to a high shelf, haven't you?"

Alice had talked with them about discipline, "Firm and consistent, but no yelling or spanking," and she explained the details of his college fund. One Saturday it had been Alice's turn to cry when she asked them if they would be his full-time parents if she died. The Saturday after that intense discussion, Alice gave them a copy of her will. Sadie had felt good that Alice trusted her to be Adam's other mother enough to put it in a legal document.

Standing at the window, Sadie waved good-bye to Adam and to Alice, too. She felt her husband's arms around her.

"Adam's beginning to look like you," she said. "He's lucky to have a good dad." Tom's arms tightened more around her.

"I didn't want to tell you until I was sure," she continued, "but I think he said 'da-da' today."

"I think he did, too," Tom said.

She turned and looked at him. "But what will he call me? He can't call two women 'Mommy.'"

Sadie hoped she did not sound angry or pathetic. She had been through all the tests, all the trying, and all the prayers. She thought she had come to terms with her infertility, but does any woman ever fully accept the harsh truth that she can never have a baby?

Tom kissed her, then said, "It's true Adam can't call both of you 'Mommy,' but God will. You have a mother's heart, Sadie, as well as a forgiving one. That's why I love you so much and why I have always loved you, and I always will."

God calls us to forgive one another as he forgives us, but sometimes the sins committed against us seem too large to forgive. That's why God reassures us that through him all things are possible. When we do not do the hard work of forgiving, a wall grows between us and the people who hurt us. Sometimes we need that wall, from a few weeks to many years, but eventually we need to batter it down with prayer. It is something we are called to do for the sinner. But the greatest benefit is to the forgiver. Forgiving frees us of the heavy burden of hate and allows us to live our lives as God intended.

Seeds of Pardon

You robbed me of my joy
And turned my smiles to tears.
Your harsh and hurtful deed
Could echo through the years.

I gave my grief to God,
And his pure, loving grace
Planted seeds of pardon
Now budding from my faith.

*H*eavenly Father, give me a forgiving spirit, one that can hate the sin but love the sinner just as you love me. Let me see through your eyes those who hurt me and help me to pray for them with love that does not count the cost. This sounds impossible for me to do, Lord, for you know my wounds are deep. I ask for your guidance and grace to love my enemies even when I have every human right not to. Amen.

*H*e that cannot forgive others breaks the bridge over which he himself must pass if he would ever reach heaven, for everyone has need to be forgiven.

GEORGE HERBERT

At Nightfall

I want to see the goodness of others,
Lord, instead of their human failings.
I want to rejoice in each encounter with
family, friends, and strangers. I want to
leave all my hurts behind so I can start
with a clean slate that counts love first
and counts it so important that there is
no room in my soul for anger. I want to
come to you tonight in praise for all the
lovely moments I spent with others today
instead of asking your forgiveness for
seeing only their failings. I know every
day cannot be like this, but just one day
will be a walk through your kingdom.
Please grant me this blessing of a day that
needs no forgiveness at nightfall.

Who's the Boss?

"Twenty thousand dollars," Karen told her friend Barb. "That's how much he has cost me in lost raises in the past four years."

The *he* in question was Luke, Karen's boss, who was working hard to get ahead in the company. He took credit for her ideas, lied about her abilities, and conveniently forgot every contribution she made until she presented proof in creative ways to management. That just made him angrier. He denied her every raise and promotion and undermined her in every way possible.

"You really need to resign," said Barb.

Karen had considered it. However, the job market was tight, and she was over 55. She had received job offers, but they required moving out of state. She loved her house and especially loved being within walking distance of her grandchildren. She had prayed and raged and was still being victimized by a man who gave new meaning to the word "selfish."

"You're not really the victim type," Barb reminded her.

"I'd rather beg on the street than whine," Karen responded.

"Keep praying for yourself and keep looking for another job," suggested her friend, "but pray for him, too."

"Ugh!"

> **Now is the time to forgive this man and help him back on his feet. If all you do is pour on the guilt, you could very well drown him in it. My counsel now is to pour on the love.**
>
> 2 Corinthians 2:7–8 *The Message*

But Barb was wise, and it would not hurt to follow her advice. Karen took praying seriously, so she confessed to God that she did not want to pray for Luke. She told God she would pray for Luke every day but not to expect her to look forward to it. It would be an act of spiritual discipline, like learning to recite the books of the Bible.

Eventually, praying for Luke became as routine as brushing her teeth. It was something she did because she'd told God she would. It was neither a bother nor a pleasure and required little thought and less time: "Lord, I lift up Luke and ask you to bless him."

Two years and many job-hunting efforts later, Luke had been promoted again and continued to block Karen at every turn. He'd cost her more money in lost raises and promotions. Nothing had changed except her attitude. Gradually, she was seeing the differences between Luke and herself. Her rage had turned to pity.

The money he had cost Karen during six years had not caused her to miss a mortgage payment or a meal. It had not prevented her from doing all the things she wanted to do, for God had blessed Karen with joy in simple things. She had never wanted expensive cars, a big house, or designer clothes. She did not need those raises to live an abundant life. Karen did not have to mistreat people to earn a living or to feel important.

Luke did, though. Strutting or stomping down the long corridors at work, he acted like he thought he was a big important cog in the corporate wheel. He rarely looked happy or even content. Karen's struggle now was with smugness and with humility before God. He did not rehabilitate Luke; instead, he opened Karen's eyes. She loved her life. She actually felt satisfaction in a job well done, no matter who took the credit.

For Karen, forgiveness came with the understanding that Luke needed someone to belittle. If not Karen, he'd find another target. Perhaps, because his behavior no longer bothered her, she was sparing his wife or a colleague from his abuse. Or perhaps God had another reason for keeping her within Luke's firing range.

Karen did not presume to know the mind of God. It was enough to know that he had given her peace and joy, an abundant life, and no fear about what one of earth's little tyrants could do to her that God would not gently heal.

Schoolyard bullies grow up, and sometimes they remain mentally trapped in sixth grade picking on fourth graders. The sensible move is to keep away from them. When that is not possible, we have to deal with them. Fighting back is the world's way, but when the bully is in power, he or she will usually win. Praying back is God's way, and it works. Do not expect the bully to change. God works in everyone's heart, but the bully might not be listening. Praying for your enemy may not change his or her behavior. It will give you insight and the ability to change the way you respond to the punches. Eventually, you will no longer feel them. It will not matter to you whether the bully knows this or not.

Willing to Try

Lord, I fail to obey your command to
"love one another" every time I remember
the cruelties that have caused me pain.
I know I need to do a lot of forgiving, but
it is so hard. All I can see is the meanness
rather than the sinking soul who feeds
on hurting others. Please help me to
understand that I am not the victim and
that with your help I can forgive. In this
forgiving, maybe I will find the strength
to love those I find unlovable. I'm willing
to try, Lord, but this is something
I cannot do on my own. Thank you
for helping me to love more and to
give more.

> Therefore, as God's chosen people, holy and dearly loved, clothe yourselves with compassion, kindness, humility, gentleness and patience. Bear with each other and forgive one another if any of you has a grievance against someone. Forgive as the Lord forgave you. And over all these virtues put on love, which binds them all together in perfect unity.
>
> Colossians 3:12–14 NIV

*F*orgiveness is the fragrance the violet sheds on the heel that has crushed it.

MARK TWAIN

*F*orgive me for complaining, dear God. Help me to remember that every time I have a headache, someone I know may have a hidden heartache; every time I don't like the food, millions have nothing to eat; every time I think my paycheck is too small, too many people have no paycheck at all; every time I wish my loved ones were not so demanding, some people have no one to love. When I look around at my blessings, my complaints seem little. Help me, God, to be grateful for my everyday gifts of family, food, and home. Amen.

Remember the Rose

Father, when I look at this beautiful world with which you've blessed us, my anger feels mean and small. What is an insult compared with a budding yellow rose? What is a rude remark compared to baby ducks waddling after their proud mother? What is being slighted compared to walking barefoot on dewy grass? Teach me perspective, and the next time anger wells up inside me let me remember the rose, the ducks, and the grass.

Nothing but Love

Amy's house was in happy disarray. In the front yard, a tall painted wood stork announced that Katie Marie weighed eight pounds, five ounces. Pink balloons tapped against the living room ceiling, and tiny pink gowns frothed out of gift boxes on the coffee table. Tears came to Laura's eyes as she watched her little sister nurse the newborn. Amy was biting her lip, concerned she wasn't doing it properly. Laura hugged her. "You're a natural mom," she assured her.

Amy smiled. "I just love Katie so much. I need to do everything right for her." She held Katie against her shoulder and gently patted her back until the infant burped.

"Wow!" Laura said. "What a big belch from such a little thing!"

"You should have heard her last night," Amy said. "She cried so loud and long, I thought she was getting colic. Finally, she drifted off to sleep and so did I. When I woke up with her in my arms, it was like we had always been together and we always will be."

The sorrow in Amy's eyes told Laura she was thinking about more than her and Katie. It was time for them to have a talk. Laura sat beside

Amy, and Amy handed her the sweet bundle of innocence now sleeping peacefully.

"You're thinking about your birth mother, aren't you?" asked Laura.

Amy nodded. She had never known her biological mother. "You know I've always hated her, from the time I was a little girl. I'd play with my dolls and tell them I'd never give them away like she did. I carted them off to college, to my apartment in Chicago; now they are in the attic."

"Katie will play with your dolls and love them," said her older sister.

"There's something you don't know," Amy continued. "The adoption agency sent me a letter from her when I was 18. She had written it right after I was born. She said she loved me too much to keep me. I tore up the letter and threw it away."

"That was five years ago," Laura said. "You didn't understand a mother's love."

Amy took Katie from Laura and held her close.

"The night after Katie was born, I wondered what I would do if I could not give her all the love and care she deserved. If I was too young or lived a life that would harm her, did I love her enough to give her up to good parents?"

"You were brave to go there," Laura said. "That's painful territory, very painful."

"I went through a box of tissues," Amy replied. "The nurse said it was postpartum depression."

"And I would have told you they were healing tears, the very best kind of tears."

Amy wiped her eyes and blew her nose. "Sorry," she said. "I just feel so bad for her. She'll never know Katie, never know I finally understand why she gave me up."

Laura let her cry, knowing that her tears were washing away a lifetime of bitterness. She got up and moistened a washcloth with warm water. She gently washed Amy's face then rocked Amy in her arms.

"That's when I forgave *my* birth mom," Laura said, "the night my first child was born."

Amy rested her head on Laura's shoulder. "And you didn't tell me. I think I know why. I wasn't ready to hear about it."

Just then the doorbell rang. Laura opened the door and hugged their mother, laden with a bag of diapers, a casserole, and yet another pink-wrapped present. Her beloved face wore a joyful look. She peered closely at Amy, and Laura sensed she was wondering if the dark clouds of bitterness were gone at last from the hearts of her two adopted daughters.

Laura took the packages so she could hold her new grandchild. "There's nothing but love here, Mom," Laura said, "Nothing but love."

Their mother kissed baby Katie on both cheeks and on top of her warm, downy head. "That's what I've been telling you both from the first moment I held you in my arms."

*G*od pardons like a mother, who kisses the offense into everlasting forgetfulness.

HENRY WARD BEECHER

"Wait till you have children of your own!" We attribute this expression to parental exasperation. Yet it is also a promise that old sins can be forgiven when viewed through the lens of maturity. Forgiveness comes with understanding. When our children cannot forgive, we can pray and trust that when they develop the heart and mind of a parent, their understanding will deepen enough for forgiveness to follow. God tells us that "sins of the parents" can wreak havoc through seven generations. By forgiving, we can stop the damage before it becomes our children's sad legacy.

*W*hat is tolerance?—it is the consequence of humanity. We are all formed of frailty and error; let us pardon reciprocally each other's folly—that is the first law of nature.

FRANÇOIS MARIE AROUET DE VOLTAIRE

Daily Challenges

God, morning dawns like a gift for me
to open and treasure. In my quiet time
alone, it seems so easy to walk into
the world with a loving, joyful spirit.
Yet I know this peace I feel now will
be challenged in many ways. I will
have unloving thoughts. I will harbor
resentments. I will speak without
thinking, and I may wound a fragile
soul. Please forgive my all-too-human
emotions and help me grow in love and
grace. With your help, I know I can learn
to be more loving and more faithful to
your word. Amen.

*L*et those who think I have said too little and those who think I have said too much, forgive me; and let those who think I have said just enough thank God with me.

St. Augustine

Chapter 10

Love Heals

Lord, daily you protect me from harm.
I feel your love surrounding me, acting as
a buffer against the world's evils. You take
my defeats and turn them into victories. You
turn my weaknesses into strengths and my
sorrows into joys. All of this you do because
I am your child and you love me. I do not
deserve your love, but you give it anyway.
Re-create your love in me. Use me to help
in the healing of others. Amen.

Lord of the Loving Heart

Lord of the loving heart,
May mine be loving, too.
Lord of the gentle hands,
May mine be gentle, too.
Lord of the willing feet,
May mine be willing, too.
So may I grow more like Thee
In all I say and do.

AUTHOR UNKNOWN

*L*ove has the hands to help others. It has the feet to hasten to the poor and needy. It has the eyes to see misery and want. It has ears to hear the sighs and sorrows of men. That is what love looks like.

ST. AUGUSTINE

I Want to Take Care of You

Amanda was in her final year of college when she noticed something was not right with her eyesight. While studying for a test, she found it difficult to focus on the print. She chalked it up to eyestrain, but later in the week when she began to experience tremors, she called her parents.

Two weeks later, Amanda was in the hospital. Her diagnosis was multiple sclerosis, a neurological disease. The doctor recommended she forget about school for the time being and go back home for treatment. Her parents agreed. She cried and wondered why this was happening to her.

Having to quit school wasn't the only thing that prompted Amanda's tears. After graduation, she was to have been married. Given the progressive nature of her disease, she had to make a decision.

When Amanda's fiancé, Jim, visited her in the hospital, she told him she would release him from the engagement. It was the hardest thing she'd ever had to do.

But Jim took her hand and said, "I love you. I don't want to be released."

"But I may be paralyzed. I'll be a burden on you," she protested.

Jim looked deep into her eyes. "I want to take care of you," he stated simply.

Amanda would remember that moment for the rest of her life. Her throat felt lumpy, and her eyes became teary. She knew then that she could get through this—or anything—as long as she had Jim.

They got married, and Amanda began an office job. For ten years, the medications kept the symptoms at bay. The couple was very happy. Then Amanda began to experience difficulty walking. The tremors became more pronounced, and her memory was affected.

Her neurologist suggested that she join a drug trial study group at a local research hospital so she could qualify for a new medication. Amanda did well on the drug, and she and Jim were ecstatic.

However, after the study, Amanda learned an alarming fact: To continue on this medicine would cost $1,000 per month. Surprisingly, her health insurance from work agreed to cover the expense. For a time, the couple breathed a little easier.

Jim kept his wife going through all her ups and downs, including the deaths of her parents. He made sure she took her medication, kept up her exercises, and got enough rest. Amanda remained an active member of her church, and her faith helped her, too. She knew God would not throw anything at them that they could not handle together. Amanda's doctor said her remarkable spirit and positive outlook on life was unusual among his patients. She gave the credit to God and to her husband.

Amanda knew that inevitably the disease would drag her down. She lost her job after 12 years because she couldn't handle it anymore. MS was affecting the nerve shields in her brain. Tasks she had once done easily now left her in confusion. Her boss was nice about it and apologized when he said he had to let her go. Amanda understood.

The biggest immediate problem this caused was the loss of her health insurance coverage. But Jim told her not to worry, that he'd take care of it. *That's what I love about him,* she thought. *He's so strong that he makes me feel strong, too.*

Although Amanda was easily overcome by fatigue, she did have spurts of energy. Being at home all day was difficult and forced her to find a hobby. She took up knitting and made dozens of scarves and pot holders.

Some good friends, realizing Amanda needed more to do, offered her a part-time job in their store. They understood those times when she suddenly ran out of energy and had to go home.

Amanda felt blessed by the people God had used to keep her active for as long as possible. Her friends at church, the support group, doctor, and friends at the shop all helped her to heal. However, at the top of the list was her husband, Jim, who had promised to take care of her and had kept his promise through everything.

*O*ne word frees us of all the weight and pain of life. That word is love.

SOPHOCLES

*D*oes God understand what it means to hurt, to be in physical or emotional pain? He sure does! Isaiah tells us of the suffering servant: He was wounded and crushed, and by his bruises, we are healed (Isaiah 53:4–5). Early Christians interpreted this passage as a reference to the Messiah who had to come, God in human flesh.

God is the expert when it comes to pain. He has endured punishment of every kind: rejection, rough treatment, physical pain, poverty, hunger, misery, war; and he will be at our side when we go through our own worst nightmares. God's love is the medicine to heal all our hurting, and the prescription is filled through prayer.

You tell us in scripture (James 5:14) that if any among us are sick we should pray over them and anoint them in your name, Lord. Thank you that we can come to you in this way and ask for your help and healing. When we call your name, may the energy of your healing power flow into our lives and make us all whole. Amen.

Prayer is the telephone call to the Great Physician, putting in motion the divine love that will bring about your healing.

Evening Prayer

Watch, dear Lord, with those
who wake, or watch, or weep
tonight, and give your angels
charge over those who sleep.
Tend your sick ones, O Lord
Christ,
Rest your weary ones.
Bless your dying ones.
Soothe your suffering ones.
Pity your afflicted ones.
Shield your joyous ones.
And all for your love's sake.
Amen.

St. Augustine

There Is a Balm in Gilead

There is a balm in Gilead
To make the wounded whole;
There is a balm in Gilead
To heal the sin-sick soul.

Some times I feel discouraged,
And think my work's in vain,
But then the Holy Spirit
Revives my soul again.

If you can't preach like Peter,
If you can't pray like Paul,
Just tell the love of Jesus,
And say He died for all.

There is a balm in Gilead
To make the wounded whole;
There is a balm in Gilead
To heal the sin-sick soul.

AFRICAN AMERICAN SPIRITUAL

Coming Back to Love

The wound had almost healed, but Dan still remembered the shock when his wife stated she wanted a divorce. She said she didn't want to be married anymore, especially to him. She threw him out of the house—his house that he'd worked for and paid for. She acted as if Dan was nothing, not even worthy of her notice. His self-esteem hit rock bottom.

Dan had showed up on his friends' doorstep, and the couple insisted he stay for awhile until he could find an apartment. They noticed he was so low that he never took his eyes off the ground.

Because Dan's wife was a member of his church, he avoided the one group that could give him the most support. His wife had raked him over the coals and tried to turn the other members against him. Dan told just about everyone he knew that he'd understand if they didn't want to have anything to do with him, but they paid no attention to that.

As it turned out, Dan's wife never returned to their church. Members assured him they wanted him to come back and continued to urge him to join them. It wasn't until the older ladies in his wife's circle came to visit Dan one day that he began to feel better about himself. They told him that as she had rejected them, too, he should return to the fold so they could all be rejects together. That broke the ice for Dan, and he returned to his congregation, assured of the members' love and support.

For more than a year, Dan's church family stood by him as he went through the legal wrangles and unpleasantness of the divorce. The support and understanding he received gave him the courage to come out of his depression and think about going on with his life.

Dan took an extended vacation to the places his wife had never wanted to visit. Camping out under the stars and breathing in the beauty of the country's natural wonders also contributed to his healing. Yet the healing was far from complete. Dan was still hurting. He couldn't get over the feeling of failure.

"Lord," he prayed, "I still don't understand how this happened. Please help me."

His friends decided to take matters into their own hands. They invited Dan and a young woman friend to dinner, telling neither about the other. Ellie, too, had felt the sting of divorce and was beginning to doubt her own worth. But both parties resented being tricked into the meeting, and they took their feelings out on each other. She provoked him with her comments, and he responded in kind. All evening they engaged in a battle of wits.

Instead of going on the defensive, Dan displayed his natural intelligence. Instead of being meek and submissive, Ellie was frank about her opinions and didn't hesitate to voice them. Their hosts looked on in astonishment as the verbal sparring continued.

Noticing the expressions on their friends' faces, the two abruptly stopped arguing and began to laugh. They declared a truce and shook hands. Dan's heart began to thaw. They soon found their personalities complemented one another. He was quiet and reserved; she was animated, open, and outspoken. She enjoyed an active lifestyle. She was just what he needed, and he thought she was beautiful.

Dan and Ellie began to date and fell in love. He began to like himself again. After a year, they married. The busy, happy couple just celebrated their 20th anniversary. They felt blessed that God had taken two bruised people and healed them with his love.

*I*n Galatians 5:13, Paul commands us to community. He tells us that we are to be servants to one another. Our motivation is the love we receive from Christ. Imagine a community in which everyone is attuned to serving one another. Real life may not be that way, but God's children are there, sprinkled among us like salt. They serve in love. These are the people who help us heal, people who—with a word, a touch, a kind deed—can soften the edges of our pain and start us on the path to healing. When you are hurting, seek them out. When others are hurting, reach out to help them. Giving and receiving in love is God's plan.

Lift This Weight

Lord, how could this happen?
My partner, my friend, my love has left
me. It happened so suddenly. My heart
is a dark, closed-up room. My grief is a
heavy stone, weighing me down. I feel
crushed under its weight and cannot
pull myself up. Lift this weight from me,
Lord. Open my heart and flood it with
your light. Replace the pain and silence
of these empty rooms with sounds of
laughter once again. Fill me with your
love so I can be whole again.

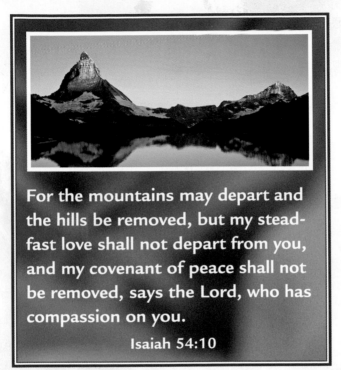

For the mountains may depart and the hills be removed, but my steadfast love shall not depart from you, and my covenant of peace shall not be removed, says the Lord, who has compassion on you.

Isaiah 54:10

*G*od does not cause your misery, he eases it. He sends you his messages of love: hands to help you, ears to listen, and hearts to share your deepest burdens.

O Love That Wilt Not Let Me Go

O Joy that seekest me through pain,
I cannot close my heart to thee;
I trace the rainbow through the
    rain,
And feel the promise is not vain
That morn shall tearless be.

GEORGE MATHESON, HYMN VERSE 3

Compassionate Father, I come to you on behalf of a friend who is shutting himself off from contact with friends and family. He says he doesn't want to depend on anyone or form relationships that may one day disappoint him. But, Lord, you have called us to community. You have shown us that loving one another and caring about our neighbor is your plan for us. Your word teaches us that we need each other and that without love we are nothing. Only you can heal the pain that causes his seclusion, but I want to help. Make me sensitive to his needs. Use me to bring your love to this lonely friend.

A Special Child

Cassie recalled the scripture about a firstborn son being set aside as special to the Lord (Luke 2:23). She held those words in her heart when her son, Peter, was born and showered him with love. She sang to him, read to him, and couldn't wait to teach him about letters and numbers and nature as she did for the children in her classroom.

Cassie had such hopes and dreams for him. She just knew he'd be the brightest and smartest child in the neighborhood. But, as her son began to grow, she noticed he didn't respond to her in the way she thought he should. She dismissed her concern as that of an overanxious, first-time mother.

When Peter's speech didn't develop normally, she began to worry. Cassie's doctor convinced her that Peter was just a late bloomer. However, it became more and more difficult to teach him routine skills like getting dressed, brushing his teeth, or tying his shoes. His attention never remained on anything for long. By this time, Peter had a little sister, and Cassie became busy with her so she didn't push Peter so hard.

When Peter enrolled in kindergarten, there were lots of holes in his learning. His teacher suspected a problem and referred him for testing. The diagnosis was intellectual disability, and Peter was placed in special classes. Cassie felt numb. Then she began to blame herself for not acting sooner. Peter's dad refused to accept the diagnosis and insisted on blaming his son's problems on the school system. In Cassie's heart, she'd known something was wrong all along, but she didn't want to believe it either.

Cassie prayed for strength, then lowered her expectations and went to work looking for all the community help she could get for Peter. She was surprised to find how many services were available. She enrolled him in speech and language therapy and sport and social activities to improve the quality of his life.

The doctor suggested they try an experimental program to stimulate and improve Peter's reflexes. It required teams of volunteers to move his limbs in specific patterns several times a day. The couple asked local scout troops, neighbors, and friends to help, and they were overwhelmed by the response. They couldn't believe so many people, even schoolchildren, were willing to help. It made them feel they weren't alone in their struggle and that God was with them.

Four teams of volunteers moved Peter's limbs in a prescribed pattern each day. At first the results were positive, and Cassie was heartened by the outpouring of love and support from strangers. But after awhile, Peter began to resist the efforts of the patterning helpers, and many of them lost interest. Cassie didn't blame them. Peter was very strong and made it difficult for the volunteers to do their work. The procedure was abandoned.

Some good came from the project, though. A neighbor family across the street had helped with the patterning, and they continued helping long after the project was over. They made friends with Peter and, in a way, adopted him. Cassie was touched by how loving and kind the daughters were to Peter. They played with him, looked after him, and protected him from the tough kids in the neighborhood who liked to taunt and tease him. They even made up original games to help him strengthen his eye muscles and coordination. When Cassie had to go back to work, the girls took turns coming over after school to baby-sit with Peter and his little sister. They showered the children with love.

By the time Peter grew up, he was very sociable. He went bowling, square-dancing, swimming, and took part in the Special Olympics. Cassie had learned to appreciate and take pride in the things her son *could* do rather than worry about what she thought he should be doing. Her son seemed very happy.

After 20 years, the family across the street were still his biggest cheerleaders, and Peter visited them almost every day. They included him in many of their family and church activities and looked after him when Peter's parents needed a night out. The daughters had married and moved away but frequently brought their children over so Peter could play with them. He always looked forward to those visits.

> For the whole law is summed up in a single commandment, "You shall love your neighbor as yourself."
>
> **Galatians 5:14**

Cassie admitted it was difficult dealing with Peter's special needs through the years, but their neighbors had stuck by them and made it easier—their love and acceptance made all the difference. She would always be grateful that her firstborn son was special to the Lord and to those who loved him.

*D*o you remember when you were a child and you would fall down and hurt yourself? Then Mom or Dad or Grandma would pick you up and kiss you, and immediately you would feel better. Now, you're hurting, but this time from fear and worry. You wonder how you can recover from the difficult situation. This is when God steps in. God sends people like Mom, Dad, and Grandma—friends, relatives, neighbors, even strangers—to touch you and help make you whole again. No matter what the hurt or whom God uses as his intermediaries, you can be sure his love is the healing force behind their care. The healing may not happen instantly, but it will happen.

And who is my neighbor?...
The one who showed...mercy.
Luke 10:29, 37

The List

I took time to pray today—

I prayed for starving children,
And God said,
"Have you fed one hungry child
    today?"

I prayed for lost souls,
And God said,
"Have you told one person today
    'I love you'?"

I was silent
Then wrote my list:
share…love…speak

$\mathcal{M}$y friend is one of the most giving people I know, Lord. She is always reaching out to help others in your name. I want to be like her, but sometimes I find it difficult to step out of my comfort zone and reach out to strangers. My intentions are good. I would like to be able to assist all within my reach who need help, but I cannot. I ask you to fill me with your love and make me strong enough to overcome my shyness, Lord. Make me willing and available to help those you put in my path. Help me discern which of them needs my help most. You have said that love is not selfish. Please rid me of any selfishness that gets in the way of spreading your healing love. Amen.

How God Answers
the Soul

It is my nature that makes me love
you often,
For I am love itself.

It is my longing that makes me love
you intensely,
For I yearn to be loved from the
heart.

It is my eternity that makes me love
you long,
For I have no end.

MECHTHILD OF MAGDEBURG

A Rift in the Family

Steve had not seen his brother, Clay, in ten years. Back then, all five siblings had come to town for their mother's funeral and stayed at the family home. The brothers and sisters had reminisced about childhood escapades and laughed over the practical jokes Clay had played on them.

Soon Steve and his sisters were hatching plans to play a practical joke on Clay for a change. Unfortunately, Clay didn't take their prank well. First he blew up at all of them. Then Steve blew up at Clay and accused him of desecrating their mother's memory. Steve didn't think of it then, but by his actions he was doing the same thing he accused Clay of. Steve apologized, but his brother didn't speak to any of them, and after the funeral he left town. Steve never heard from him again. He hadn't realized how emotionally fragile Clay was.

Through the years, Steve and his sisters kept in touch. They repeatedly sent birthday and Christmas greetings to their brother and tried to phone him, but he never responded. Steve felt terrible. It hurt to think he could talk about loving your neighbor in church on Sunday, yet he couldn't patch things up with his own brother.

Feelings of guilt hovered in the back of his mind. Then Steve became ill with cancer. He longed to talk to Clay and experience the camaraderie they'd once had. If he was going to die, he at least wanted to make things right with his brother.

When Steve began to recover, his wife urged him to go see Clay. They got in the car and drove 300 miles to his brother's house. Steve circled the block twice, passing Clay's home both times. The couple ended up staying at a motel that night and driving home the next day. Steve couldn't face another blowup and rebuff.

A few more years went by. Every time Steve and his sisters got together, they talked about Clay and their regrets, but no one wanted to face Clay's fury again so they did nothing.

Then Steve heard that his brother was facing serious surgery. He desperately wanted to know how Clay had fared but heard no more news. That summer, Steve made up his mind to go back and try to see his brother again.

"Lord, help me to go through with it this time," he prayed.

He called his brother. Clay came to the phone at his wife's urging, and he agreed to get together.

When Steve and his wife arrived at his brother's home, they were met with reserve. The two men did get to talk about Clay's illness, though. They had a good, if not warm, visit, but it was a start. Clay's wife made lunch, and Steve kept trying to avoid mentioning things that would upset Clay. They parted on a cordial note, and Steve felt relieved that they had made contact again after ten years.

Gradually, the other siblings took turns visiting their brother and mending fences. The next year, Steve went back to his hometown and heard rumors about his brother "acting strangely." A neighbor reported that Clay and his wife had come home for a visit in the spring, and Clay had seemed confused about where he was.

Once again, Steve contacted his sisters, and they confirmed the rumors. Through further investigation, Steve found out his brother was in the early stages of Alzheimer's disease. Steve went to see Clay again, and they talked about the things they had done when they were kids. It was like old times. Clay had forgotten all about their differences, and Steve felt as if he had his brother back again at last.

Steve went home and prayed. He thanked God that they could talk again before the disease completely robbed his brother's mind of its memories. And Steve thanked God for making their love stronger than their differences.

Redeeming Love

When people are rejected, Lord, they begin to doubt themselves. They see themselves as unworthy of love. Self-loathing is destructive, and sometimes I get that feeling, too. That's when you come and speak directly to my heart: "You are my child. I love you. You are royalty!" Then I am restored. Thank you, Father, for your redeeming love. Amen.

A mobile of the "fruit of the Spirit"
(see Galatians 5:22–23) was hanging in
my church sanctuary for an entire year.
From my place in the choir loft, I read
the words every Sunday, yet I could
never remember all nine of them. I
couldn't seem to get past the first one:
Love. But that isn't a bad thing, I tell
my conscience, because all the others
spring from love. When we exhibit joy,
peace, patience, kindness, generosity,
faithfulness, gentleness, and self-control,
we are spreading love. To spread love is
to heal. Just think of it: Your joy, your
patience, your gentleness, even your self-
control, can be loving, healing acts.

Savior, Teach Me Day by Day

Savior, teach me day by day,
Love's sweet lesson to obey;
Sweeter lesson cannot be,
Loving Him Who first loved me.

Teach me thus Thy steps to trace,
Strong to follow in Thy grace,
Learning how to love from Thee,
Loving Him Who first loved me.

Thus may I rejoice to show
That I feel the love I owe;
Singing, till Thy face I see,
Of His love Who first loved me.

JANE E. LEESON

How wonderful, O Lord, are the works of your hands! The arch of the sky displays Your handiwork. In Your love You have given us the power to behold the beauty of Your world robed in all its splendor. The sun and the stars, the valleys and the hills, the rivers and the lakes all disclose Your presence. The roaring breakers of the sea tell of Your awesome might, the beast of the field and the birds of the air bespeak Your wondrous will. In Your goodness You have made us able to hear the music of the world. The voices of the loved ones reveal to us that You are in our midst. A divine voice sings through all creation.

TRADITIONAL JEWISH PRAYER

ACKNOWLEDGMENTS.

Page 195: "I Arise and Go Forth" from *Science of the Mind* by Ernest Holmes, copyright © 1938 by Ernest Holmes. Copyright © renewed 1966 by William M. Lynn. Used by permission of Jeremy P. Tarcher, an imprint of Penguin Group (USA) Inc.

Page 236: "The Gleam of Faith" from *What God Is Like* by James Dillet Freeman. Published with permission of Unity Books, Unity Village, Missouri. Copyright © 1973.

Unless otherwise noted, all scripture quotations are taken from the *New Revised Standard Version* of the Bible, copyright © 1989, by the Division of Christian Education of the National Council of the Churches of Christ in the United States of America. Used by permission. All rights reserved.

Scripture quotations marked NIV are taken from *The Holy Bible, New International Version*. Copyright © 1973, 1978, 1984, 2011, International Bible Society. Used by permission of Zondervan Publishing House. All rights reserved.

Scripture quotations marked NASB are taken from the *New American Standard Bible®*. Copyright © 1960, 1962, 1963, 1968, 1971, 1972, 1973, 1975, 1977, 1995 by The Lockman Foundation. Used by permission.

Scripture quotations marked LB are taken from *The Holy Bible, New Living Translation*, copyright © 1996, 2004, 2007 by Tyndale House Foundation. Used by permission of Tyndale House Publishers, Inc., Carol Stream, Illinois 60188. All rights reserved.

Scripture quotations marked *The Message* are taken from *The Message*. Copyright © 1993, 1994, 1995, 1996, 2000, 2001, 2002. Used by permission of NavPress Publishing Group.

PHOTO CREDITS

Cover images: Art Explosion, Photodisc, PIL Collection, Shutterstock.com

Art Explosion, © Sharon K. Broutzas, © Henry G. Nepomuceno, Photodisc, PIL Collection, Shutterstock.com, Thinkstock